D1706533

THE GRADUATE THEOLOGICAL FOUNDATION

Paul Tillich in Conversation

"psychotherapy ... religion ... culture ... history ... psychology"

James B. Ashbrook

Edited with Introduction

Wyndham Hall Press

PAUL TILLICH IN CONVERSATION

Edited with Introduction
James B. Ashbrook

(Published by special arrangements with the
Graduate Theological Foundation of Indiana.)

Special appreciation for permission to use materials
previously published in these pages goes to both
Foundations and *The Journal of Pastoral Care.*

Library of Congress Catalog Card Number
88-040118

ISBN 1-55605-038-0 (softcover)
ISBN 1-55605-039-9 (hardback)

With deep appreciation to

GRANVILLE, OHIO

-- its First Baptist Church as a place for ministry
-- its Denison University as a place for inquiry
-- its community as a place for relatedness

PAUL TILLICH IN CONVERSATION

INTRODUCTION

For those who know little about Professor Paul Tillich, this book will introduce them to both his ideas and the kind of person he was. For those who are already familiar with him and his work this book will remind them of what he was like and the way he thought. In either case, this book is a liberal education in itself as it weaves together the warmth of his person with the range of his insights. (More technical and systematic material is available in *The Thought of Paul Tillich,* edited by James Luther Adams, Wilhelm Pauck and Roger Lincoln Shinn. New York: Harper & Row, 1985.)

It was a long stretch -- from Friday noon through Sunday afternoon -- that Reformation Weekend in 1960. Yet time flew by even as it seemed to be suspended. So much conversation, so much sharing, so much searching, so much celebrating. The occasion was the visit of theologian Paul Tillich to a little college village in central Ohio: Granville, the home of Denison University. Two full days of talk -- theological talk -- a feast for the soul. Most of all, a time of presence as a community opened its heart and mind to one who opened his own mind and heart to the life of God in the lives of people.

In these pages are the conversation with Professor Tillich carried on with psychotherapists and a liberal arts university faculty. This was a familiar experience for him, one in which he had engaged all his professional life. (Hannah Tillich, *From Time to Time.* New York: Stein and Day, 1973, pp. 132, 144) The distinguishing component this time was that it occurred in a relatively communal setting with sophisticated but mostly unheralded people.

Each talk fest focused on a particular theme in the style of his correlational method: psychotherapy, history, culture, psychology. I have only added notes to clarify information about his comments which might not be familiar to the reader. Most of the material is ordinary Tillichian observations, but the conversational style makes his thinking more accessible to the nonprofessional theologian and personally searching person. The discussion of theology and psychology represents a classic statement of his which is both synthetic and critical. Those acquainted with D. MacKenzie Brown's *Ultimate Concern: Tillich in Dialogue* (New York: Harper & Row, 1965) will feel in familiar territory as to both style and content. The chief difference, however, is between his responding to undergraduate students and his talking with university faculty.

The sharing with professional psychotherapists, however, represents unique Tillichian material. As an item of interest, when Wilhelm and Marion Pauck were researching their then projected two volume work on his life and thought, Professor Pauck raised the question with me about the exchange in which Dr. Tillich speculated as to whether historical theology was even a possibility in the light of apparently symbolic activity on the part of individuals completely isolated from the Christian tradition. Professor Pauck went on to indicate that nowhere else had Tillich expressed himself in print so explicitly about the issue. (Wilhelm & Marian Pauck, *Paul Tillich: His Life & Thought* Volume 1: *Life*. New York: Harper & Row, 1976, p. 235)

Tillich's friendships with psychoanalysts is well-known. (H. Tillich, op. cit. p. 143). From 1940 to 1945 he met monthly with the New York Psychology Group. (Pauck, op. cit., pp. 222-223, 320; Adams, Pauck & Shinn, op. cit., pp. 105, 107-111) Among its members were anthropologist Ruth Benedict, psychiatrist Gotthard Booth, psychoanalysts Erich Fromm and Rollo May (Rollo May, *Paulus: Reminiscences of a Friendship* [New York: Harper & Row, 1973]), and Jungian analyst Frances G. Wickes. Tillich's memorial tribute at the service for neo-Freudian Karen Horney

(*Pastorial Psychology*, 54, No. 34, [1953], pp. 11-13) and Erik E. Erikson's tribute at the memorial service for Tillich himself (*Harvard Divinity Bulletin* 30, no. 2 [1966]) indicate the quality of his associations with those engaged professionally in working with human psyches in depth.

In one of his final public appearances before his death on October 22, 1965, Tillich appeared with psychologist Carl Rogers before cameras of Radio/Television at San Diego State College. That unusual dialogue was recorded, broadcast and published. ("Paul Tillich and Carl Rogers: A Dialogue," *Pastoral Psychology*, Vol. 19, No. 181, February [1968], pp. 55-64) The conversation in this volume, however, came five years earlier when he was still vigorous. Moreover, it is the only record available of what the content of such a discussion between psychotherapists and the eminent theologian might consist. There is, however, a record of his historic conversation with the noted Zen philosopher Hisamatsu Shin'ichi, which took place in the autumn of 1957, in Cambridge while Dr. Shin'ichi was a Visiting Professor at the Harvard Divinity School. ("Dialogues, East and West: Conversations between Dr. Paul Tillich and Dr. Hisamatsu Shin'ichi (Part One)," *The Eastern Buddhist*, Vol. IV, No. 2, [New Series] October 1971, pp. 89-107; (Part Two), Vol V. No. 2 [New Series] October 1972, pp. 107-128; (Part Three), Vol. VI No. 2 [New Series] October 1973, pp. 87-114)

How did this "event" come about? And surrounding the actual give and take of the conversations, what were some of the human interests aspects of the occasion?

For the reader interested in this more personal material I share something of what led up to the occasion and some of what went on throughout the weekend. What I write about now is, inevitably, a very personal account of what Professor Tillich meant and means in my own personal and professional life. In telling about him I am, of course, telling about myself.

HOW IT CAME ABOUT

Every starting point, I suppose, is arbitrary. I could begin with my invitation to him to come to Granville as we stood on the runway of the Cleveland, Ohio airport in April 1959. And I want to tell you about that exchange. But first let me go back to a late spring day in 1951, for that is the moment I remember in which my heart and mind quickened in response to this man and his opening up the power of the Christian tradition to my inquiring soul.

I was attending the New York Annual Conference of the Congregational Christian Churches in Irondequoit, New York. As a way to be present but uninvolved, I sat in the balcony of the church where the meeting was held. I was completing my first year in parish ministry, feeling somewhat drained and in need of spiritual nourishment. Although I realize the necessity of institutional structures, I have always been restive with sitting through business meetings and pouring over committee reports. In an effort to put that time to something constructive, I picked up a book I had brought as a way of escape if the occasion proved too deadly. Since the occasion did leave me bored, I opened the cover of Tillich's *The Shaking of the Foundations* (New York: Charles Scribner's Sons, 1948) and began reading.

The first chapter, "The Shaking of the Foundations," spoke directly to my view of the world's agony. Soon I came upon the chapter "You Are Accepted." The title leapt out at me. That experience has been shared by countless others. Here was a theologian speaking to my heart as well as to my mind. Here were liberating words, the good news of the gospel that takes my own limited and limiting self and frees me to live in the power of the future. (See Pauck, op. cit., p. 93 for Tillich's own experience of the sermon and its meaning. His wife Hannah's book, op. cit. is a painful description of some of the demonic forces at work in his and her psyches, which would have contributed to the power of this message for himself.) I felt ecstatic as I left the balcony and went out into the fresh air.

I had become aware of Tillich in seminary. But my seminary, Colgate Rochester, was in upstate New York, somewhat removed from the vibrant immediacy of metropolitan New York. His *Protestant Era* (Chicago: The University of Chicago Press, 1948) was out, and I had studied it in a seminar which introduced me to his method of correlation. The dynamic dialectic between questions in the human situation and answers from theological truth felt exciting, though abstract. But his sermons were different -- so different in fact that they made me want to devour everything he had written.

Even more, that encounter quickened in me the hope of studying under him directly. I had no expectation of doing scholarly work with him or of becoming a Tillichian expert. Rather, I looked to him as one who could open for me the power of the Christian tradition and the dimension of depth in myself and in others. I was a pastor of a parish, a minister to people struggling to cope with the crippling effects of culture and the constricting consequences of religion. And Tillich stood on the boundary between the conventional and the creative -- for me as for many others. I was aware of his critics, those who claimed that he was unChristian and a threat to genuine religion. (Pauck, op cit,. pp. 167, 176; e.g. Nels F. S. Ferre, "Tillich's View of The Church," in *The Theology of Paul Tillich,* edited by Charles W. Kegley & Robert W. Bretall, pp. 261-265. New York: Macmillan, 1952). But for me -- for my own personal life as well as for my professional responsibility -- he represented a liberating way of thinking and talking about what matters most in human life, namely, our ultimate concern.

So, for the next few years I read all the Tillichian material I could find. With a graduate fellowship from my Divinity School, I was able to spend a year in New York City. That period was a rich mixture for me. I served as the first pastoral counselor intern at the then American Foundation of Religion and Psychiatry and now The Institutes of Religion and Health, while being enrolled in the program in applied psychiatry for the ministry of the William Alanson White Institute of Psychiatry, with Rollo May as my advisor. That February, Tillich lectured to a standing room only crowd at the Institute. I entered into intensive psychoanalytic psychotherapy as part of the program but, more importantly, as a necessity for myself if I were to be a more authentic human being and a more effective minister. And, with all that, I was a special student at Union Theological Seminary on Morningside Heights.

It was Professor Tillich's last year before he "retired" to Harvard and then to The Divinity School of the University of Chicago. In the summer of 1954, he lectured on "Religion and Culture." During the academic year he presented the last three sections of his systematic theology: Existence and the Christ, Life and the Spirit, and History and the Kingdom of God, (see Pauck, op. cit., pp. 232-245 for a description of the comprehensive complexity and persistent complications of "The Systematic Theology") and I sat in the front row of every lecture. I savored putting together his ideas with his presence. I understood more of what he was saying because I was experiencing something of the power of his presence (cf. May, op. cit., pp. 25-36). An informal photograph of him lecturing in that classroom hangs just inside the door of my office. Again, I am not unique in that depth of appreciation. Nor is my experience of him as a formative figure in my life something that only I have known. We all have those to whom we look and from whom we derive strength. But for me, that year and my chance to hover on the margins of his activity were significant.

Two events remain vivid in my mind:

> For his "Culture" course I wrote a paper on "The Impact of The Hospital Situation on Our Understanding of God and Man [sic]." He responded quite positively to my attempt at a correlational approach to pastoral care. I had identified and described the dominate experience in the hospital situation of one of brokenness and the dominant concern as one for wholeness. His response encouraged me to submit the paper to *The Journal of Pastoral Care,* which published it. (Vol. X No. 1, Spring

1956, pp. 1-15; later included in *Religion and Medicine,* edited by David Belgum, pp. 61-80, Ames, Iowa: University of Iowa Press, 1967) Some chaplain supervisors in Clinical Pastoral Education referred to it through the years because it utilized theology as one stood in the midst of human need.

A more personally significant time came as I followed through on a suggestion by Rollo May. At his urging, I was investigating "The Functional Meaning of the Soul in the Christian Tradition" in an attempt to break out of the trap of Cartesian dualism which separated body and soul. (Rollo May, "Psychotherapy, Religion and the Achievement of Selfhood." In *Liberal Learning and Religion,* edited by A. N. Wilder, pp. 315, 312. New York: Harper, 1951). He wanted me to talk with both Tillich and Reinhold Neibuhr about the topic.

Neibuhr was recovering from his stroke but still engaged issues and students with vigor. He was quite clear what I needed to do: Read Augustine's *De Trinitate,* Roger Williams' *The Bloudy Tenet of Persecution,* Jonathan Edward's *The Freedom of The Will,* and Johs. Pedersen's *Israel.* And, of course, I read his own *The Nature and Destiny of Man.*

When I asked Tillich the same question, his response was entirely different, naturally. He rose from his chair and began pacing his cluttered office, holding his head in his hands and muttering more to himself than to me, **"Ach, I vanted to spend ten years on the subject!"** With that he had nothing more to suggest. For him, the whole loomed so vast in its implications that he was unable to focus on a single suggestion.

I do not recall ever being with someone who seemed so in the grip of existential anxiety as he gulped in great drafts of air. (cf. May, op. cit., pp. 28-30) Years later I came upon his wife's description of the phenomenon: "Paulus lived in fear. His nervous body was tense; his desires many. His fingers would fiddle with a pebble from the beach, a silver coin, or a paper clip. He breathed unevenly and signed heavily, an ever guiltridden Christian in distress." (H. Tillich, op. cit. p. 24) I eventually managed to get enough of an understanding of the issue of the phenomenological fullness and mysterious depths of centered self-awareness and transcendence, which the concept "soul" was used to identify, to have a version of it published in *The Journal of Pastoral Care* (Vol. XII, No. 1, Spring 1957, pp. 1-16).

At the end of the academic year I returned to parish ministry, this time in the First Baptist Church of Granville, Ohio. In those days that parish served as a meeting place for much of the town and gown interaction. About sixty percent of our worshipping congregation consisted of college students. Yet, Granville was also like most small towns -- one main street with four churches on the corner, plus a couple of smaller congregations scattered around the edges of the community.

The larger community and state capital of Columbus lay 30 miles to the west. Upon my arrival in Granville, I sought contact in the wider area, more particularly the Columbus State Hospital and Psychiatric Clinic. Richard Johnson, M.D., directed the clinic and eventually developed a psychiatric training program in the hospital itself. He, along with Vincent O'Connell, his chief psychologist, myself, and Harvey Guthrie, minister of St. Luke's Episcopal Church in Granville, met together every Friday afternoon for a year. We explored mutual interests in the interface of psychotherapy and ministry. During the years that followed, that association and collaboration deepened.

In the spring of 1958, Dr. Tillich gave the Rauschenbusch lecture at Colgate Rochester Divinity School, my seminary which is located in the city in which I had served my first parish. The title "Between Utopianism and Escape from History" (*Colgate Rochester Divinity School Bulletin*, Vol. XXXI, No. 2, May 1959, pp. 32-40) suggests his exploring the struggle in Germany to find hope after World War I. (See also Tillich, *On The Boundary*, op. cit., pp. 32-36; Adams, Pauck & Shinn, op. cit., p. 59). The other lecturer for that convocation was Rudolf Bultmann. ("What Alienates Modern Man [sic] From Christianity?" Ibid., pp. 18-31). There was no way I could not <u>not</u> attend.

Tillich was magnificent as usual. I remember an arrogant pastor challenging him as to the irrelevance of his thought for children. And Tillich's response, as I had experienced his responses throughout his classes, was an open transforming of hostility into healing. He had a way of turning the most absurd or disruptive question into an opportunity for exploration in depth. (H. Tillich, op. cit., p. 114). On that occasion, he went on to elucidate about the theological profundity of children as they ask their "why" questions and participate in an imaginative engagement with bewildering reality.

The convocation ended, and I arrived at the airport to return home to Ohio. As I entered the door of the large four engine plane, I found myself in a deserted cabin. Only one passenger was there -- and that passenger was Professor Tillich! What an opportunity to talk with him personally, but what an intrusion upon his privacy. I felt I could not sit in the seat beside him nor was I prepared to put many rows between us. As a compromise between the desire of my heart and the constraint of my conscience, I sat in the seat directly across the aisle from him, nodding as I did so, but saying nothing.

When the stewardess came along, he asked for help. He explained that he was traveling to Columbus and had to change planes in Buffalo. Furthermore, he got very confused in airports because he could not understand the announcements over the loudspeaker system. Could she suggest how he might make the transfer without difficulty?

Here was my chance for contact! I leaned over and magnanimously said, "Dr. Tillich, I am flying to Columbus also and have to change in Buffalo. I would be happy to help you make the transfer." He expressed relief, the stewardess went her way, and I leaned back in quiet excitement. Nothing more was said during the twenty minute flight, but I looked forward to the prospect of sharing a few hours with him.

The Buffalo airport was not the greatest attraction in those days. Like most centers of transportation, it had long passage ways and small waiting areas. Dr. Tillich appeared weighted down by his heavy brief case, so I suggested that I carry his, since I was younger, and that he carry mine, since it was lighter. In the exchange he commented about the fact that both his wife and his doctor badgered him about not lugging so much weight all the time. Eventually we found a quiet area and settled in for the wait.

In the course of our becoming more acquainted he noticed a large poster on the wall. It pictured Mexico City. "I visited my friend Erich [Fromm] there," he casually remarked. "An ethicist through and through but no ontology!" (See Pauck, op. cit., p. 258).

We got to talking about theologian David E. Roberts who had died in the spring of 1955. Though much younger than Tillich, he had been a close personal friend, a sympathetic interpreter, and a "staunch ally" (Pauck, op. cit., pp. 167, 174). I shared a dream I had had at the time in which I saw the central staircase of the seminary collapsing. In response, Tillich warned how too much psychologizing can have tragic consequences, as in Roberts' case. He had suffered from severe neck pain for months, attributing it to a symbolic stress which was "a pain in the neck." It turned out to be a terminal condition which could have been treated if it had been diagnosed earlier. Years later I learned that Roberts had sustained him during the period in which Tillich's existentialism was attacked so heavily by their colleagues at the seminary (Ibid.) His death accentuated the painful reality of illness for Tillich. The need to heal, quite understandably, became the theme for his final commencement sermon at Union when he urged the graduates to "heal the sick, cast out demons." (Ibid., p. 248)

And so our conversation went -- a mixture of personal associations and stimulating reflections about theology and culture. I simply savored our time together.

We had another change of planes in Cleveland. Neither of us had anticipated that. As we stood on the runway waiting to board a third plane, I suddenly found myself asking a clearly calculated question.

"How do you decide to accept a speaking invitation?" For the first time I realized that this might be a kairos for me in terms of getting him to Granville.

"Easy," he replied immediately. "First, importance. The Rauschenbusch lecture was 'important.' Second, friendship. And the third is money."

Without thinking I blurted out: "I will give you $500 if you would spend a weekend in my parish and an extra $250 to spend Friday afternoon with a group of psychotherapists."

In those days $750 was a respectable sum of money. I had no idea where I would get it, but get it I would . (See Pauck, op. cit., for his concern about a limited income in retirement [p. 247] and his insistence that he never accepted any money if he were "invited by student groups or churches without a large budget." [p. 253]. See H. Tillich, op. cit., for his difficulty with fees and the "top money" he received for lecturing during later years, [p. 199])

Tillich did not even hesitate. With his own spontaneous generosity and enthusiasm he tapped me on the shoulder and said softly, "For **you** I vill do it!"

I was unclear whether he would do it because of importance, friendship, or money. No matter! I was ecstatic. he told me to write his secretary, who would work out details. In retrospect I realize I had taken to heart a comment of his after that long wait in Buffalo. As we had settled into our seats of the next leg of our flight, he had remarked with earnestness, "You have been a physical and spiritual blessing to me." I am still awed at the fact that in carrying his brief case, in helping with his confusion in the airport,and in sharing time together I had been a "blessing." I was experiencing what his wife Hannah called his "genius for friendship." (H. Tillich, op. cit., p. 218)

During the last leg of our flight I outlined what I thought would be a stimulating but not exhausting time for him in the parish. He need not lecture. In fact, I preferred his simply talking with groups of people, letting them ask questions and encouraging him to respond. This format helped him to be more accessible than any other. I had seen it and I had experienced it. That was what I suggested. Finally, I wondered if he would be willing to preach at an all-community worship service. So our planning unfolded.

As the plane arrived at the gate in Columbus, what turned out to be an officious delegation from a nearby university rushed out on the runway to greet him. He was scheduled to lecture there, and they were getting anxious. But I was still relishing our contact. I asked if he would be willing to meet my wife and children who I knew would be at the gate. With characteristic delight, he pushed past the delegation explaining that he had to meet **my** family before he went with them!

My wife hardly knew what was happening. There she stood waiting for me with our three children -- seven, five and one -- at her side. As I swept up, I managed to stammer, "Honey, I want you to meet Dr. Tillich. Dr. Tillich, this is my wife, Pat, and my children, Peter, Susan and Martha." His response was one of presence and interest, no mere formality. He told her how helpful I had been to him on the trip and how much that meant.

Eventually, the delegation whisked him off, appearing offended that anyone else would have the audacity to interfere with their guest.

The task of negotiating a weekend proved more difficult than I had anticipated. This period found him at the very height of his fame. In 1955, he accepted the invitation of Harvard's President Nathan Pusey to become University Professor. (See H. Tillich, op. cit., pp. 197-203, for a description of the Harvard period.) The Pauck's characterized this last decade of his life from 1955-1965 as "The Ambiguity of Fame," (Pauck, op. cit., pp. 246-285) while for him and Hannah it was "harvest time." (H. Tillich, op. cit., 202.) He was on the road lecturing so frequently that *Time* magazine referred to him as a "wandering" professor. Stung by the implications, he wrote a letter to Pusey on "22 December 1960" explaining his activities.

In the course of the letter he indicated that he turned down "at least ninety percent of all invitations," which his secretary reported as averaging in some weeks "15-20." (Pauck, op. cit., p. 254) Nevertheless, because of his commitment to me, his secretary persisted in working out the visit.

He would come after his trip to Japan. It would be Reformation Weekend. What a fortuitous combination -- immediately following his exposure to Japan, and more especially Zen Buddhism, and in connection with the anniversary of our Protestant tradition.

Arrangements fell quickly into place. The Board of Higher Education of the American Baptist Churches contributed money to cover the cost. The small intimate group of psychologists readily chipped in to cover the expense. Churches in the village were responsive and the college receptive. All was in order. Then, in the summer of 1960, I accepted a position in pastoral theology at Colgate Rochester Divinity School. We moved to Rochester, but the planning went ahead. On Friday, October 28, 1960, I picked him up at the Columbus airport. The visit had begun! Years later

I learned that during that October and November he had been "engaged . . . every weekend," which meant we had added to "his ferocious schedule." (Ibid, pp. 254, 255)

The actual conversations make up the substance of the book. However, just as I have described what led up to the event, so I want to fill in some of the personal exchanges that occurred during the event.

WHAT TOOK PLACE

My seven hour drive from Rochester proved uneventful. But once he and I made contact the momentousness of his presence and the incisiveness of his comments converged. As we walked toward my car, I was, of course, carrying his heavy brief case. We reminisced about the previous occasion.

I was driving a four year old Ford station wagon, and had parked it next to a new luxury car of some kind. He started toward that car. I quickly said, "No, Dr. Tillich. I'm sorry but this one is mine." "Sorry," he retorted. "Vhat do you mean you're sorry? Vhy do you apologize?" In one short exchange he had opened a deep undertow in my life -- a feeling of needing to make excuses in order to justify simply being around.

The sun shone, the air felt fresh, the leaves looked lovely as we settled down on the screened in back porch of Dr. Johnson, my psychiatrist friend and colleague. There were ten of us all told, including Tillich: three psychiatrists, one of whom was a German woman emigrant; three clinical psychologists and one psychiatric social worker with special interest in Fritz Perls and Carl Jung; and two clergymen. He understood he was simply to be present in an informal give-and-take on issues growing out of psychotherapeutic experience. His recent visit to Japan loomed fresh in his mind; the group's interest in Zen added to that focus. Dr. Johnson took the lead in exploring issues, as I have identified in the transcript.

Topics ranged from the experiential orientation of Zen in contrast to theological abstractness, through individuality and relatedness, selfishness and self-love, to guilt and guilt-feelings. The most intense exchanges explored whether the Christ symbol was necessary for forgiveness and whether people could forgive themselves. The pivotal and poignant point came exactly where Professor Pauck had found it, in Tillich's wondering about the psychological power of the symbol of the cross and whether the actual event of the cross was necessary for forgiveness to be received.

> "Why has the symbol had such an immense impact on the consciousness of people?" he asked the group.

> "The question that is most important for me is whether this same psychological power can be produced by meditative self-acceptance without the relationship to the symbol of the cross. . . . What is the symbol of forgiveness in the ground of being itself or in the power of life itself if it is not the cross? I try in my theology to reinterpret the cross in this sense of that one does not need to make his [or her] assurance dependent upon the event, as a sacrificial, substitionary suffering and this whole Anselmian idea. I think this is really almost impossible for us today."

After some exchange he returned to his concern.

> "How can this [acceptance] be expressed in the same convincing way as that which really produces, which has produced, which still produces [it] in innumerable people, the conquest of their uneasy conscience? Can we have another symbol for it or, at least, another experience? . . . I would be greatly relieved because I know how infinitely difficult it is to understand all these terrible associations [related to the cross event] -- what you called the whole scene of miracles around it. We must get rid of this, of course. How is it possible?"

We had been talking long and hard, but the issue of the cross event and the cross symbol for the experience of forgiveness haunted him.

> "This is a very important discussion for me, because I really see how difficult it is -- even to reinterpret the symbol in this modified form 'as manifest [in Christ]' instead of 'because of [Christ].' If this is gone, there is no other symbol."

We kept talking even though our time was up. All agreed with him that this had been "a wonderful discussion."

Our thirty mile drive to Granville was a time for recalling the ideas we explored and for relaxing from the stimulating exchange. The major part of the schedule lay ahead -- conversation with the faculty of Denison University. Throughout the weekend he revelled in the fall splendor of the nestling hillsides. In walks between buildings he stopped every little while to drink in the splendor of the trees, indicating he had not expected to see such beauty.

Except for the fourth conversation, which had the specific theme of "Psychology and Theology," the other three were shaped completely by the interests of the group. The thematic titles are my attempt to give some organization to what, in fact, emerged in a remarkably organized manner. He began with his appreciation for not having "to make one more speech." And he went on to remark that he thought "sometimes the old Platonic dialogue is more fruitful than anything else." With that the talk began in earnest:

> "I have difficulty understanding a statement you made, Professor Tillich, which says that religion is the substance of culture and culture is the form of religion. Could you explain what you mean . . . ."

Dr. Tillich voiced his ambivalence between making a speech in response to such an "embracing" question and his "own preference for dialogue." He restrained the extent of his response, but the pattern of curiosity and clarification had begun. The questions unfolded with impressive specificity:

> "Would you expand on what you mean by a Christian culture?"

> "Would the high Middle Ages be such a culture?"

> "[You have made] a statement to the effect that of all the styles of the history of Protestantism, the twentieth century style in visual arts is best able to express the human condition as Christianity sees it. Could you elaborate on this in view of the fact that symbols have become personal and that art in general today is nonfigurative and makes no reference to the real world?"

> "Is there a chance for a return to a sacramental-confessional church with . . . concern for the totality of the . . . human community . . . and yet without the dogmatism and the authoritarianism that Rome represents?"

Thus went the talk which focused the group on the theme of "Culture and Religion." Three more sessions followed.

The second discussion continued the theme of culture but with a more theological focus. Immediately following the break in the evening's program, Dr. Tillich was asked to develop newer trends and points of emphasis which might be more satisfying to him than the extreme alternatives between liberalism and neo-orthodoxy. Someone wondered why there could be a via media "only if you have gone to extremes . . . [and] maybe the via media is a way of saving them from having to go to the extremes." After identifying the importance of the "historical method" in approaching matters of faith, Tillich described the struggle to find meaningful liturgical forms, including the quest for community, in the face of Protestant individualism.

By now the discussion had shifted from more standard questions and answers to more probing exchanges.

"Mr. Tillich, how would you apply this deliteralization [as shaped by Bultmann's method of demythologizing] to a view of the Eucharist that would embrace the real presence?"

"Dr. Tillich, you said that we needed to find an answer to the problem of this fragmented society. Through your concept of the New Being, are you suggesting . . . that each individual can become a new being through his[or her] total involvement in society?"

The evening ended with his comments about the dimension of the eternal in the face of nuclear destruction. That set the agenda for Saturday morning which focused on the theme of "History and Theology."

The conversation began with a question about "kairos as the critical point or the fulfillment of time in history," the major kairos of the Christ event, and "derivative kairoi." What would he say are "some of the kairos points in our present world era?" He went on to describe the situation he experienced in Germany following World War I, the rise of religious socialism, and the quality of a subjective consciousness of living in "a moment where the times must be interpreted with a prophetic spirit." (See Pauck, op. cit., pp. 70-75; also Paul Tillich, *The Socialist Decision*. Translated by Franklin Sherman. Lanham, MD: University Press of America, 1983)

Questions persisted about the danger of subjectivism and ways to avoid it. How could the concept of "kairos" be an interpretive tool that the historian could use? The cyclical view of history -- from an archaic past through an autonomous criticalness to a theonomous fulfillment -- had been exposed as an example of "European provincialism." Have other peoples and religious groups, then, "discovered Christ . . . even though unheard of, using a different terminology. . . .?" That turned attention to the encounter of world religions with each other and the encounter of religions with secularism in Asia, Africa, and Russia.

During the break in the conversation, issues of nationalism continued to be explored. Characteristically, Tillich picked up and expanded on the negative meaning of "ism" in German, in contrast to English. (Hannah, his wife, provides a powerful description of his clash with the rising Nazi forces and the necessity for their leaving Germany in 1933 [H. Tillich, op. cit., pp. 148-156].) Thus, in German, "every 'ism' is a negation -- is a distortion -- of something. . . . Psychology is good. Psychologism is bad," he concluded.

This last formal period had been designated specifically to deal with issues of "psychology and theology," in part, because of my own interests, in part because I had been a bridge between the departments of religion and psychology at the University during my pastorate there, and in part because Professor Parker Lichtenstein, then dean of the University, was a sophisticated behaviorist with broad and deep intellectual interests.

The Dean started the discussion in a formidable but straight forward manner: "What do you mean by freedom and destiny as a description of the determining and creating powers or activities of [human beings]?" From this definitional orientation the questions shifted to distinguishing between anxiety in its destructive and constructive expressions. In response to a question about Gestalt psychology, Tillich linked that with his "philosophy of life . . . [as] the function of centeredness, of integration, and the continuous fight with disintegration."

Building on these first three themes, someone wondered about the relationship between the New Being as a conscious context and the therapeutic process. Tillich's description of the four dimensions of a whole person -- bodily, sociological, psychological, and ultimate -- led to one person's speculation as to whether the rejection of "the concept of an immaterial, immortal soul," in contract to concern with conditions of living and with behavior," was "a gain or a loss...?" With characteristic candor, Tillich rejected "this almost materialist doctrine of a soul-substance beside our body substance."

The next question proved to be "four questions" -- each related to aspects of the power of being overcoming the estrangement of non-being. In concluding his long response, he insisted upon the centrality of the mystical element in religion in contract to religion being merely a system of moral commands. Someone in the group appeared to seriously disagree, which Tillich perceived and immediately said that he "would like to hear your criticism of this." But the time was up. We stopped for lunch. Yet even then he continued to respond to eager inquirers.

Much of the luncheon conversation was centered on art. Picasso's "Guernica" was only 50% Protestant, while Grunewald's work was totally Protestant. (See Pauck, op. cit., p. 78) Bosch's portrayal of humanity in the center of the picture of the Garden of Delight portrayed the diagonal dimension coming down from the divine to the demonic and the other dimension from the tree to the animal. He spent much of the afternoon with a German scholar talking about Tillich's associations with the literary and artistic communities in Germany in the early 1920's. (See Pauck, op. cit., pp. 57-93; H. Tillich, op. cit., pp. 115-120, 123-135, 141-156; Adams, Pauck & Shinn, p. 142) He reported revelling in the contact.

For myself and for many in the parish and community, the occasion not only celebrated Professor Tillich's visit but also my return after having moved away five months previously. The reunion was special -- so special that I described the weekend at the time as "forty-eight hours of Pentecostal presence." The struggles of the past were suspended; the joys and sorrows since my leaving were shared; love and loss, hurts and hopes fused in a joyful presence; we were experiencing a timeless ecstasy of being together.

A small dinner was held for Tillich at the home of the Dean of the University. I arrived later than the other guests. People were engaging him in animated conversation. As I entered the living room, Marian, the hostess and wife of the Dean, rushed over to greet me as I rushed forward to greet her. We threw our arms around each other -- one of a wonderful series of such greetings. Then, as she and I stepped back to welcome one another further, she suddenly became aware of the fact that Dr. Tillich was sitting there taking all this in, and, in her mind, he probably was wondering what was happening. She turned to him and explained our behavior with the comment, "He was our former pastor, you know."

One of the guests, Mary Kay Campbell, was an artist of some reputation as well as a member of the Art faculty. She had done two woods prints and a water color piece, which to my eye expressed Tillich's three kinds of authority: autonomy or self authority, heteronomy or imposed authority, and theonomy or transcendent authority. I wanted to test my interpretation by inviting his responses. First of all he appreciated her original style, which for him reflected religious style. While he identified each picture with the patterns as I had, and even though all three he regarded as within the life of God and within our own lives, and even though he chose the wood print which manifested theonomy as the best of the three pieces (a confirmation of its having won a prize in a regional art show), he could not live with such a reality. For him it lacked the aliveness and conflict of the other two works and so was too resolved.

> Tillich provided his own elaboration of living "between heteronomy and autonomy" in his little volume *On the Boundary: An Autobiographic Sketch* (New York: Charles Scribner's Sons, 1966, pp. 36-45). Because of the early death of his mother he found "outbreaks, often extremes, were necessary" in order "for the maternal side" of his makeup to express itself. Consequently, [c]lassical composure and harmony were not part of my heritage," he wrote. ". . . the theory of dynamic truth, which holds

that truth is found in the midst of struggle and destiny, and not, as Plato taught, in an unchanging 'beyond'" is what accounted "in part for certain premises underlying my interpretation of history." (pp. 14-15)

Sunday morning broke bright and clear. As people crowded into the sanctuary of the First Baptist Church, it seemed as though every barrier in the community was being transcended. People of every religious persuasion -- Jewish, Catholic, Protestant, atheist -- came. People of every socio-cultural background gathered -- poor and rich, educated and uneducated, rural and urban, town and gown. People of every age appeared -- high school students and retired professionals. For a moment in its history the entire community gathered as a community of those who cared ultimately about what matters most in life. Church walls had disappeared, and, like the New Jerusalem, there no longer was any temple, for God had become all in all (Revelation 21:22).

He preached on the subject "Forgetting and Being Forgotten." Later it appeared, with minor revisions, in *The Eternal Now* (New York: Charles Scribner's Sons, 1963, pp. 26-35). He lifted up the questions of what we forget and what we remember, as well as what we "should" remember and what we "should" forget. In closing, he admonished us to "push into the past and forget that which should be forgotten forever; and . . . go forward to that which expresses our true being and which cannot be lost in eternity."

Intriguingly, the Paucks ended their study of his life and thought with an excerpt from this sermon. They regarded the words which follow as "his most fitting epitaph:" (Pauck, op. cit., p. 285)

". . . in the anxiety of having to die is the anxiety of being eternally forgotten.

"Is there anything that can keep us from being forgotten? That we were known from eternity and will be remembered in eternity is the only certainty that can save us from the horror of being forgotten forever. We cannot be forgotten because we are known eternally beyond past and future." (Tillich, *The Eternal Now*, op. cit., p. 34)

At lunch he expressed excitement about the liturgy of the service itself. He had been impressed by the prayers in that there was nothing of the conventional and much of the meaningful. For that reason I include the text of my pastoral prayer:

"They that wait upon the Lord shall renew their strength. They shall mount up with wings as eagles, they shall run and not be weary, they shall walk and not faint." So let us unite our hearts in prayer.

Holy God, Thou who art the life of our lives, the strength of our strength, the love of our love, Thou are closer to us than we are to ourselves, and yet Thou dost remain a mystery to us. We go forward and Thou are not there, we turn back and Thou has left.

Give us courage, O God, to live in the present -- in this moment, in this place -- that we might truly know that we are Thine and Thou has not forgotten. O God, to seek Thee is to see ourselves, to be painfully reminded that we have failed to become what Thou hast meant us to be; that in our distance we have become aloof, and in our closeness we have absorbed one another until there is nothing left.

We have scarred the glories of Thy world with the tragedy of our lives. We have emptied Thy firmament of Thy glory and filled it with a mushrooming cloud of our own destructiveness.

O God, break through our defensive shells, free us from our fear, enable us to find warmth in our closeness and depth in our distance. Restore us to our rightful minds, enable us to find our proper usefulness that with Thee

> as our Lord, and one another as companions, we may press on toward the goal of the prize of the high calling in Christ Jesus our Lord.
>
> In this moment, O Lord, we pause that the deepest longings of our hearts might become known to each of us in our own ways before Thee. . . .
>
> O God, hear our prayers, Amen.

Most of all, Tillich voiced excitement about the response to the reading of the Word. For years, he indicated, he had lectured against the phrase "May God add His Blessing to the reading of these words." Here, at last, he heard a positive and existential response, namely: "If you respond to these words, then for you they have become the Word of the Living God."

The luncheon was only for university students. The room was crowded, though intimate. Their questions allowed him to share, it seemed to me, more of himself and less of his knowledge.

One sophomore asked why she needed the church. Couldn't she have the Presence of God without it?

With a quiet softness he gently led her from the public space of corporate worship to the private space of her heart. He explained that he could not have preached the sermon he had without having received the Word, the hymns, the theology, the tradition. Suppose, he suggested, that he were to come to her in her dormitory room and talk with her. Would she have all the richness of the ages locked up in her own little heart. No matter how large her heart was, it simply was not big enough to contain the hymns, the prayers, the tradition, the theology of the ages.

Another asked him to define the Holy Spirit.

He began by defining the meaning of definition. It requires circumscribing an area. The fourth section of his systematic theology on "Life and The Spirit" developed the idea that Holy Spirit meant the dynamic uniting of power and meaning. However, it had come to mean "ghostly images." He went on to describe an assistant he had had in Germany when he was a lecturer there and how, upon returning to Germany after the war, there was the same assistant much as he had been years before. For him, the entire situation felt like he was seeing a ghost -- the same chair, only with the leather cracked and broken and the wood splintered from Allied bombing. But the Holy Spirit has no such association with such ghostly images.

Was he, another asked rather naively, an example of the New Being? His response could be expected. If he said he was an example of the New Being, then, of course, he was not a manifestation of the New Being. The word "Christ" means the bearer of New Being. Pictures of the saints are not of men [and women] who do magic but rather those who are transparent to the divine presence. Thus, they are pictured as having little devils surrounding them with pitch forks. These are not imps running up and down, but rather a powerful symbolization of demonic forces within the unconscious. The saints remained open to the demonic, while at the same time overcame that in the power of reconciling love. (See H. Tillich, op. cit., pp. 23-25 for a brief, but powerful description of the Tillichs' own struggle with the demons and the demonic in themselves.)

In returning to the airport late Sunday afternoon, I found myself falling back into the same apologetic stance with which we began. Hadn't it been a burden for him to come? Yes, he acknowledged, there was a tragic element in every decision. He found it hard to say "No," even though his doctor, his wife, and his secretary all told him to stop traveling so much. But he felt like an evangelist. In addition, his coming had been an expression of his personal desire to respond to what I had done for him.

In turn, he kept apologizing for making so much trouble for me, especially my having had to drive all the way from Rochester. He found it hard to realize that my meeting with him and being there were neither work nor burden for me. I would not have missed a single moment. Unexpectedly, for me the event pulled together my ten years of personal and professional life. All the normal barriers were down. There had been an intensity of openness which must be similar to that experienced at Pentecost. In a strange way, the weekend would not have come in such numinous power if I had not left Granville. In some unexplained way, my leaving had released the constricting side of our unconscious forces of identification, even as Jesus had to go away in order for the disciples to receive the Comforter (John 14:25-26).

The intensity of each presence can never be sustained. However, Pentecost provides a criterion by which to evaluate what is going on in all events. Because it happened, the lack of presence is experienced but without such overpowering alienation as before. A breakthrough has come by which to judge and live through each moment. So now the hope in every situation, I have come to understand, is to release the full presence of being. And we can be present, to some extent, even though it will never be in that crystallized fullness. The events of a weekend with Paul Tillich did not make presence possible. Rather, presence was manifest, seen, known, experienced in a fullness that had been going on and would continue to go on.

One final vignette. Some months later I learned about an exchange and its aftereffects. Professor Tillich had been housed at a bed and breakfast home of a retired missionary couple from India. As he was leaving, the woman gave him a bag of applies "for Mrs. Tillich." Some more sophisticated people of the parish were chagrined when they learned of it. Tillich, I was told, had been his usual gracious self. A few months later he was lecturing at The Divinity School of the University of Chicago and, in the course of informal remarks, began speculating upon the ontology of the apple!

FROM PRESENCE TO PRINT

I kept the tapes and cherished the memory of those two days. When the MacKenzie Brown *Ultimate Concern: Tillich in Dialogue* (op. cit.), appeared, I began to think about sharing the material. After he died in October 1965, I was talking with Roy W. Fairchild, Professor of Christian Education at San Francisco Theological Seminary. He urged me to pursue the possibility of publication.

Will Davison, then Editor of Religious Books for Charles Scribner's Sons, responded to a letter of inquiry with keen interest. We corresponded during May and June of 1966, as I was preparing to spend the summer in Granville, while teaching in a National Defense Education Act program for counselors at The Ohio State University. With strong encouragement by him, I began the laborious process of transcribing the tapes. Further, I got clearer about the possibility of the task.

The Brown dialogues lacked footnotes, thereby losing some of its possible value. So, I would include notes: something relevant from his sermons and autobiographic material, from his writings that dealt with a particular issue, references to the issue in his systematic theology, and references from the two critical interpretive works about his thought (Kegley & Bretall, op. cit.; and Walter Leibrecht, Ed., *Religion and Culture: Essays in Honor of Paul Tillich.* New York: Harper & Brothers, 1959).

Part of my motivation came from the experience of his genius for combining the existential and the abstract but the difficulty of keeping the specifics in mind. David Roberts had reported how he was always "mystified as to how [Tillich] could be so flexible, concrete, vital, and 'close to home' on the one hand, and so schematic, abstract, abstruse, and remote on the other . . . it is a weird experience," Roberts wrote, "which I have undergone many times, to have problems answered with great sensitivity and patience, by being brought into connection with some relevant segment of the system, only to discover later that I do not happen to be the man who carries this system around in his head." (David E. Roberts, "Tillich's Doctrine of Man [sic]." In Kegley & Bretall, op. cit., p. 130)

At many points in the text of the conversations I wanted to provide background information that would identify the context out of which he was making a point. Such referencing, I suggested, would lift the significance of the volume from that for a general reader to the level of that of scholarly interest.

I tentatively titled the volume *Tillich in Conversation: Apologist in Action.* With that in mind I intended to write a final chapter using the material to illustrate the apologetic task which he exemplified throughout his life. (Adams, Pauck & Shinn, op. cit., pp. 14-19) He had indicated that his Systematic Theology "was written [with the] intention [of being] the apologetic discussion against and with the secular." (Paul Tillich, *The Future of Religion.* Chicago: The University of Chicago Press, 1967, p. 91) And in dialogue with Brown's students he had stated that "I presuppose in my theological thinking the entire history of Christian thought . . . and I consider the attitude of those . . . in doubt or estrangement of opposition . . . And I have to speak to them. My work is for those who ask questions. . . . For the others, I have the great problem of tact." (Brown, op. cit., p. 191) For him, the crucial issue in the apologetic task "means to defend oneself before an opponent with a common criterion in view . . . the court of judgment where the dispute can be settled." (Tillich, *On the Boundary,* op. cit., p. 60)

The process of referencing his comments and allusions turned out to be an education in itself. I found myself searching for what to me were obscure names, places, and practices. Entirely new vistas of knowledge opened up as I reengaged his ideas and his involvements. The project was proving to be a labor of love, and what better place in which to undertake it than in Granville where the event had occurred.

On Christmas Eve, 1966, Davison telephoned to say that Scribner's had signed the contract. We were on our way into print! What a Christmas present that was. I had expressed concern about securing permission to publish the material from the literary estate, and the publishers had indicated there would be no problem. But a problem there was! The estate refused permission. It had already projected several posthumous pieces, and this would detract from these. Furthermore, it was second rate Tillich. However, the estate did agree to allow me to publish the conversations in journal form.

With that decision, I stopped the extensive referencing with Tillich's other works. I did, however, continue the contextual references. The material here is virtually the same as that which was published. I have made only minor corrections, along with using inclusive language. Reference to his visit to Japan, however, have been updated. At the time I had no acquaintance with Zen Buddhism, Japan, or people associated with him in those connections. Since the publication, I have had the privilege of spending three weeks in Japan. During that time I was able to talk with several Zen and Christian scholars in connection with research on a book of my own, *Humanitas: Human Becoming and Being Human* (Nashville: Abingdon Press, 1973).

In the course of these contacts I visited Professor Masao Abe, then of Nara University of Education. Professor Abe has had a distinguished and varied career of presenting the Kyoto School of "doing" philosophy in the United States and Europe. (See Frederick Franck, Ed., *The Buddha Eye: An Anthology of the Kyoto School*. New York: Crossroads, 1982, pp. 61ff) We discovered that we both were influenced deeply by him and his thought. (Masao Abe, "Christianity and The Encounter of the World Religions [Review Article]," *The Eastern Buddhist*, vol. 1, No. 1 [New Series] September 1965, pp. 109-122; *In Memory of Dr. Paul Tillich*, Ibid., No. 2, September 1966, pp. 128-131) As we compared experiences, I learned that Professor Abe had helped arrange his visit to Japan in 1960, especially the part which included Kyoto and Nara. (See

Pauck, op. cit., pp. 258-261; H. Tillich, op. cit., p. 200; and Adams, Pauck & Shinn op. cit., pp. 197, 211-212, for a description of the visit.) We chuckled over Abe's excitement at Tillich's visit to the ancient capital of Nara and Tillich's greater excitement at the prospect of an evening with some geisha girls and subsequent disappointment at discovering what a stylized and formal event it proved to be. (See H. Tillich, op. cit., pp. 175-177 for a description of the Tillichs' fascination with Red Light districts.) The revised footnotes reflect knowledge which I acquired as a result of my visit.

Nothing more developed about the material until the winter of 1987. Dr. John H. Morgan, Senior Fellow and President of the Graduate Theological Foundation, and I were discussing theological education. In the course of the conversation we discovered our mutual appreciation of Dr. Tillich. Dr. Morgan expressed an eagerness to gather the separate journal articles together for publication in a single piece. With that encouragement we began the process -- I to writing an introduction of a more personal sort without the analysis of Tillich as an apologist and with an updating of the notes, and he to securing permission from the literary estate. For permission to publish this material, I am most grateful to Mutie Tillich Farris, current executor and to Robert C. Kimball, the former executor of the literary estate who gave the original permission for the material to be published in journal form, and to the *Journal of Religion and Health, The Journal of Pastoral Care,* and *Foundations* to republish the conversations.

In reflecting upon this introduction I am aware of two by-products. The first is a strong impression that, except for some of the demonic aspects of his own psychodynamics, the material gives a fairly accurate picture of Professor Tillich as a person. This impression has been reinforced as I have found and identified similar experiences in other sources. And the second is that the material gives a fairly accurate introduction to his thought and style of engaging issues. Thus, I would locate this material between the powerful existentialism of his sermons and the compelling discussions of his smaller books. Even the coherent essentialism of his systematics is accessible through these modest windows into the largeness of his mind and soul. Tillich would recognize and appreciate the characterization and quality of the volume. I am grateful to him for enlarging my life and faith.

October 1987:

The 22nd anniversary of his death
The 27th anniversary of his visit
The 101st anniversary of his birth

THE EXPERIENTIAL, THE THEOLOGI-CAL AND PSYCHOTHERAPY[1]

THE EXPERIENTIAL

Zen Buddhism

Visit to Japan[2]

Question: Did you have a change to speak to some of the Zen[3] people there?

Dr. Tillich: Oh, that was my main object in going. I had continuous discussions with the Buddhists who are partly professors of philosophy, partly priests, partly monks, partly Zen masters, including one archbishop and his son, whom I knew before, of the so-called True Pure Land sect. This is the largest church in Buddhism in Japan.[4]

Question: Do you feel they have something to say to us?

Dr. Tillich: Yes, at least to me. If the concepts of being and non-being are not taboo as they are in most of American Protestantism, then we can have very profound discussions with them.[5] If it comes to the ordinary American concept of social activity -- Kingdom of God as a religious symbol, and so -- then it is much more difficult. But they agree now that they are lacking in this.

Question: This other dimension?

Dr. Tillich: Yes, the horizontal dimension. We can agree with them in many respects in the vertical dimension, very little in the horizontal dimension.

Dr. Johnson: I have been interested a little in Zen, mainly from its relationship to psychotherapy and particularly the way in which they try to teach by non-direction -- in a sense -- where the teacher tries to help the pupil to become open to [oneself] without outside aid. . . .[6]

Dr. Tillich: I know, you mean the kind of teaching of the Zen masters which is not real teaching. It is introducing the student into the attitude of Zen -- the whole "sitting" process,[7] which is the discipline preceding any enlightenment. Oh, of course, we presupposed this whole realm. I mean, I knew Suzuki, who was here.[8] I had many discussions with him in New York. I knew Hisamatsu, who is a real Zen master, one of the greatest.[9] This [background of understanding] was presupposed. Then we tried to go more to the fundamentals.

Of course it [teaching by non-direction] can happen to you. When I visited Suzuki in Kamakura, Japan, and asked him the question, he refused. He said something, "Suppose I am not disposed to answer this now?" This was a riddle word. Of course, he did not want to be impolite. He invited us -- Mrs. Tillich and me -- to a wonderful dinner. It was the method -- not to do it on the basis of a mere abstract discussion.

Dr. Johnson: This has been a thing for me. I have been interested in it because in many ways, psychotherapy is a problem of how to help an individual to become acquainted with [oneself]. [One] certainly cannot do it by dealing with abstractions about life.

* * *

THEOLOGICAL ABSTRACTNESS AND ZEN BUDDHISM

Question: Something that bothers me in Christian theology is the attempt -- instead of theologizing with respect to the actual experience situation -- to set up theology as abstract principles and concepts. Do you think Zen can have a real effect upon Christian theology in terms of returning it, maybe, more to a description of growth such as mystical theology in the Middle Ages?

Dr. Tillich: Yes, it is the form in which many Western people take in Asiatic mysticism. It is the nearest form because it was deprived of some Indian ascetic and negativistic characteristics by China. When Buddhism went to China, it experienced a change.[10] It was the kind of practical emphasis of the Chinese attitude generally towards life in all its religions that influenced it. So when it was brought to Japan, it was not the genuine Indian Buddhism; it was a practical one.[11]

Question: Do you know Hannah Colm?

Dr. Tillich: Hannah Colm is one of my oldest friends.[12] . . . Now she is very much impressed by Zen Buddhism. She was in Japan the three months before I was there. She largely knew similar people. But she went much deeper into the reality of Zen than I did. She was "sitting" for a week. "Sitting" is a name for the meditative attitude in Zen Buddhism. They simply call it "sitting" in the English translation. I do not know what the Japanese word is.[13]

She had real experiences and deep understanding of it. In a talk with Hisamatsu, the Zen master, he told her that she really is able to talk to him on an equal footing; while he said to me -- in Cambridge where we first met -- that I am still away from the Kingdom of God, or in Buddhist terminology, I have not reached the state of Enlightenment[14] because I still accept the idea of evil -- of good and evil as contrasting things. . . .

CONTRASTS BETWEEN CHRISTIANITY AND ZEN BUDDHISM

Enlightenment vs. Kingdom of God

Dr. Johnson: That was an interesting thing for somebody to say, isn't it? I mean, this comment that you said was made to you, that you had not reached the Kingdom of God?

Dr. Tillich: No, not reached Enlightenment, he said. Kingdom of God is not a good word -- that is only the German phrase, or the words of Jesus that the particular questioner is not far away from the Kingdom of God. For them, this is individual Enlightenment. This is all that they have.

Question: There is no community in it?

Dr. Tillich: There is no community in it. It is the direct relationship to the Ultimate.

Question: Does this damage their capacity for inter-relationships?

Identity vs. Community

Dr. Tillich: You ask a very discerning question -- because our discussions went to that point rather frequently. Perhaps I can tell you of one discussion which was with a priest of the Shingon sect.[15] This is not a Zen sect. They call it sect; you can call it churches. There are large churches. They have nothing to do with sects in the technical sense. There we came to the concept of substance -- in the sense of standing upon oneself, substantia being something which can stand, which underlies something else, and therefore is not changing in itself but is based upon itself. In this sense, the priest, who was also a scholar, said that if the individual human being has a substance -- that means is standing upon [oneself] as a separated person, as we would say, probably, in English -- then no community is possible.

I answered him, if the individual is not this, then only identity is possible but not community. This was really a point at which the difference came out very sharply. For them, the concept of identity is the highest. Even the very beautiful way in which they exercise compassio - compassion -- is based upon an identification with the other one, but not in participation in somebody who is also something quite different -- that is, an individual in [one's] own standing.[16] These ideas are very far away from them.

Dr. Johnson: I think I could begin to raise some question as to the worth of the Ultimate that they could reach -- or a thing like that -- because it certainly takes communion, in a sense, between people or the encounter with people out of their ultimate state, then.

Dr. Tillich: Yes, and, I mean, the real difference is: has the individual person, as individual person, an ultimate meaning? They would deny such ultimate meaning because for them the highest is the formless self.[17] Formless self is the difference between subject and object and the self-consciousness has disappeared. Then, of course, the individuality as such has disappeared. [One] is one beside another one, but [one] is not an individuality. There are the main differences, which have great cultural consequences of course.

Question: Would that not have consequences in analysis, too, then?

Dr. Tillich: Yes, therefore, I am very doubtful whether one can do what Fromm and Karen Horney try to do -- to bring Zen Buddhism into psychoanalytic thinking. What I know about the psychoanalytic purpose is to set people free from their compulsive limitations -- to give them the freedom to act creatively now as individual persons. If this is so, then, I would say, in guiding them into Zen Buddhism after this would somehow eliminate the aim of setting them free. Of course, you can say, "We set them free to sit, to mediate, and to become one with the Absolute, then." But you would not set them free for action, for living in this world.

Dr. Johnson: That is the thing I think about. At least I believe, from my own experience in working with people, that probably the last thing a person finds in [oneself] is some true capacity to love. I think this concept is basic in Christianity, too. This attitude of theirs certainly pushes Zen and Christianity miles apart. Their highest level would be to be practically incapable of relatedness with other human beings. I think that maybe, in our point of view, the highest capacity is ultimately to be able to relate, because that is a part of being human.

Overagainstness

Dr. Tillich: Now this is true in theory -- what you say -- but it is, interestingly enough, not true in practice. I have never received so much considerateness in my life as in Japan. This is a part, at least, of love. It is based on the concept of compassion, but compassion is not simply in contradiction to love. The people -- some of the colleagues, for instance -- were really almost saints in the way they related, but they did not do it in terms of agape. They always did it in terms of compassion. Therefore, they usually do not dare to criticize -- to contradict, and so on -- which (action) belongs to agape, the Christian meaning of love, but it does not belong to compassion.

Comment: So there is not a set over-againstness.

Dr. Tillich: Exactly. Neither psychologically nor critically, morally nor religiously. But the side of compassion in love -- the feeling-in-the-place-where-the-others-are -- we have that in the New Testament, too. Jesus had compassion with the masses. So it is not an anti-Christian concept, but it is not the full concept. He also threatened the masses. That, I think, a Buddhist would not do.

Dr. Johnson: I begin to see what you mean. When it comes right down to the kind of people, maybe there is not so much difference. it is in the way we conceptualize it.

Dr. Tillich: It is very hard to make the difference, but I would say the difference is the positing-against each other. That is the real point.

Question: The over-politeness?

Dr. Tillich: Yes, but it is not only politeness. It is really a kind of identification with the other one.

Comment: You are me.

Dr. Tillich: You are me. That one is me because in you is the same Buddha as a <u>scintilla</u>, as a spark, as it is in me.

Selfishness and Self-love

Dr. Johnson: In a sense, we have the same problem in a popular understanding of Christianity which tries to elevate selfishness to the ultimate goal of self.

Dr. Tillich: Now this brings me to a struggle I have with Erich Fromm -- about this concept of self-love. He rightly makes the point that there is a necessary and justified self-love over against the selfishness which does not really love itself but is a greedy and self-disgusted kind of working. Now this is one of the most illuminating things I have learned from him.

Be careful about terminology, I said to him, I would not like to use the term "self-love," because you must always add -- which Augustine already had to do[18] -- the right self-love and the wrong self-love. So why not use different terms and do not use self-love at all. Why not distinguish three types of relationship to oneself:

> the natural self-affirmation, which every human being has and which, in the New Testament, is called loving the other one 'as oneself.' This is presupposed. This is not a commandment. Every living being has a natural

self-affirmation. This is not denied in these words of Jesus. Let's call it self-affirmation;

the negative form of self-affirmation. If it turns against the others and uses the others as means, then it is selfishness;

and then, the highest form of self-love. It is to affirm oneself in spite of not being able to affirm oneself. That I would call self-acceptance in the accepting the unacceptable, namely, oneself.

Now these are three words which I suggest be used instead of the very ambiguous word self-love.

Dr. Johnson: I know in trying to teach Fromm's concepts to psychotherapists, I had to modify the language because I could not teach by using self-love. I did something similar to what you did, but I only took the two -- selfishness (Yes.) as opposed to self-respect, which is to care what happens to one's own self. (Yes. Yes.) You start throwing the term self-love in, and it is just not received in terms of what Fromm was trying to communicate.

Dr. Tillich: Yes, self-respect is still another form which would partly belong to the natural self-affirmation -- partly to the higher form of self-acceptance. But I think we need a better terminology there.

Problems in Terminology

Dr. Johnson: Well, I don't know. I think maybe what we need is no terminology -- in a sense of having to have new names. I mean everything we are talking about in psychotherapy -- really -- are things which have been talked about since time began. Why everybody has to coin a new language. . . . Oftentimes you can use a language, but the thing is that you have to get concepts down to some simple terminology before the term that you are trying to use conveys anything.

Dr. Tillich: Yes. At least I think the best is to give examples of what your concept means -- to make constellations. I think that is important. If you do not want to make definitions, which is often impossible, you can illuminate the term by putting it into constellation with other terms. That is a way illuminating it -- not in an Aristotelian definition of having a higher genus, then a middle concept, and so on, but instead of that, relating it to other concepts.

There are some concepts which cannot be defined: "being" cannot be defined; "meaning" cannot be defined. You always presuppose (the reality) when you define it. "Freedom" cannot be defined, but it can be put into constellations.

Dr. Johnson: This is particularly true, I think, in trying to tell somebody who has not had the experience what psychotherapy is (Yes.). . . . My favorite phrase is to say it is like trying to define the flavor of a strawberry. You could write about what a strawberry tasted like, but nobody else would know, anyhow, until they tasted one, probably. In psychotherapy, I find that often times I am fighting concepts in psychiatric residents in order to try to remove the concepts so they can allow themselves to have an experience instead of filtering it through a conceptual framework which separates them in a sense from early experiences.

Dr. Tillich: But how will you teach psychotherapy except by examples which are then conceptually interpreted?

* * *

THE THEOLOGICAL

Comment: I am curious how that concept of "all a [person] needing to know being built in him [or her] someplace" would fit in with what Zen taught. It must be the same because they are working all the time to get a person to experience [oneself] aren't they?

The Paradoxical Nature of Acceptance

Dr. Tillich: Now first of all, I would not say that the acceptance is built in. The acceptance is always paradoxical. There is the psychoanalytic acceptance, which is similar to the acceptance in friendship, relationships and family relationships. All this is a limited acceptance. Then there must be the universal power of acceptance -- let me say -- by life itself where the analyst and the patient are in the same boat, because the analyst needs it as much as the patient needs it -- the ultimate acceptance. There the Christological problem comes in, I mean, because of Christ as the symbolic expression that God accepts us.

Christ Symbolizes Acceptance

Comment: You mean that Christ externalizes this natural rationale of acceptance?

Dr. Tillich: No, I would not call it acceptance. Acceptance is always paradoxical. It is not natural. Natural self-affirmation is what is usually called self-love -- in an indifferent way, not good, not bad, but natural.

But then, to be aware of one's estrangement -- distortedness or so -- and, nevertheless, to accept one's self is a paradoxical thing, which cannot be produced by ourselves intentionally. It is something different. It needs both the power of the community, which has ultimate sources, and then, finally the ultimate power itself in order to enable somebody to accept himself [or herself].

I know how difficult this is from the point of view of the psychoanalytic situation -- to overcome the self-disgust, self-hate, self-escape, and all this. But it can never be in the ultimate dimension of human life. Then we need self-acceptance which can only be given by life itself or by the ground of being itself. Here, I would say, Christ is the symbol.

So, I would have answered this question in this way. I would have said, acceptance and Christ crucified are not simply separated, but they are not the same. The question is not whether acceptance is built-in or whether it comes from an event like Golgatha. The question is that acceptance is built-in in the essence of God -- if you want -- I mean, in the ultimate ground of our being. That we accept acceptance is paradoxical for us. This paradox is manifest and at the same time resolved in the cross of Christ.

There in the cross you can see it in a way which is psychologically very difficult to interpret. Why have people always seen divine forgiveness in the cross? But suddenly, it has happened to them. The theories the Church used to interpret the event are very miserable. They are not sufficient. I think that one day psychoanalysis should help us interpret the feeling of peace and being atoned and [the experience] of sins being forgiven, which come to people from the vision of a faith in the cross of Christ.

Is the Christ Symbol Necessary?

Comment: But does this experience of acceptance need the Christ event to be real?

Dr. Tillich: Now the Christ event is another problem. What has really impressed people and has produced the Anselmian Theory of atonement[19] is that [God] has carried our sins as an exchange in terms of satisfaction and all that. This is not the image of the cross, I mean, which we have in a thousand things. The event itself is the source out of which this image comes; but if it comes as such an image, it is interpreted. [The meaning] was not immediately manifest in it [as seen in the fact that] the disciples ran away. They did not even see the crucifixion. Later they interpreted it in this way.

There is one thing in these theories of atonement which is always very dangerous. We forget that according to the Bible and some theology, in my opinion, God is [The One] who reconciles and not Christ who enables [God] to do it. This is a very bad theory, I think, as if God is dependent on Christ. But Christ manifests what God is always doing or is willing to do or is ready to do in this event.

Comment: So that this event simply shows us what is going on constantly at all times, in all places?

Dr. Tillich: In God, of course. But it shows it in a way which is a criterion. I mean, I would say that the way in which it is shown in the sacrificial cult in the Old Testament, for instance, or in other religions, is not sufficient. There is something lacking. While the description of this event shows all moments which make it possible, the event I would say (shows it) definitely.

I do not know the psychological answer. I have often tried to find the answer: why are people who see the cross reminded by a physical cross of the event of God's attitude toward us? Why are they grasped so much that they are convinced, "yes, this means the forgiveness of sins?"

Comment: Because they need it so much.

Dr. Tillich: Yes, but why do they concentrate on this [event]? Why is this helpful and other things are not? In Buddhism there is no such thing at all. In Judaism there is God's grace as a promise which is behind the experience of forgiveness, but it is not such an event. So, why is [the cross event] necessary?

Comment: Was not the cross that important a symbol in the very early years of Christianity?

Dr. Tillich: Oh yes, of course. It was in Paul.

Comment: From the beginning?

Dr. Tillich: It was not painted in the early years. In painting it appears only in Rome in the fourth century and not earlier.[20] But it was presupposed.

The oriental Church, immediately, took the resurrection as the central symbol, because of the Greek idea of light and life -- Christ as the bringer of immortal life and the bringer of illuminating light, these two things. There the cross does not play a great role, but it does in the Apostolic message, I mean, in the New Testament. It does, then, again in the Roman Church. Therefore, in the sarcophaguses of Rome there is the oldest sculptural root -- that is, the presentation of the cross.

Comment: Well, would not Jung say, I cannot speak except in terms of what Jung says here, that there are certain kinds of experience or ideas -- I do not know quite that word -- certain human experiences that can only be expressed because there are, say, not words for them. Needs or wishes could be expressed only in certain ways. As an example, the cross for a Western society -- namely, us in a Christian way now -- would stand for or symbolize the possibility of forgiveness of sins and redemptions. In a way, it would be more than just a symbol, because it can be a very immediate experience of resurrection. Somehow there could be the possibility of redemption.

This is possible for us in this way because it is, he says, a collective unconscious. Now this sounds like a very tricky metaphysical term, but it make sense. I actually had someone yesterday who is working through this whole thing. In a fantasy this is what he withdrew to -- a cross. The cross was filled with light; and he was afraid to touch it, you see. So June says that these things appear in people's experience, and this is only one way they can express them.

Dr. Tillich: Now the collective unconscious is a term which I use myself when I speak of symbols. I think a symbol is more than "only" a symbol. A symbol participates in the reality of what it symbolizes, and, therefore, it has power. But what kind of power?

In this sense of symbols I consider the cross a symbol. It is actually a symbol of God's participation in the suffering and sin of the world. That is the way in which Paul has interpreted it, finally, for the Christian Church.

But you need the historical event, the consequences, and all this.[21] You could not derive the meaning of the symbol for the collective unconscious if the historical event of the cross had not come. Because it has come, the collective unconscious has positively received it. The reception of an event by the collective unconscious is a process which I would like to understand, because you have brought in some concepts -- some interpretive concepts -- such as redemption and so.

Comment: I always like to think of it in this way -- anyway for myself -- as sort of a dialectic. What could take its place? What other thing could stand in its place -- supposing what this experience expresses or does for us? What could be put in its place? I have never been able to think of anything.

Dr. Tillich: But even so, if you say this, why do we need anything at all? Why is the simple message "God has forgiven" not enough? This is the riddle for which I want to have -- always have wanted but never got -- a little bit more light from the psychological side.

Comment: I know for myself I do not need it. I do not need it because I am much closer to -- somehow -- the Buddhist way.

* * *

Comment: We agree, or do you agree, that there is nothing that is to be forgiven or that there was nothing that needed to be forgiven in the first place?

Dr. Tillich: No, I would not agree with that. That was the reason Hisamatsu told me that I am not yet Enlightened, because I said, "There are things to be forgiven and continuously."

* * *

Dr. Tillich: Now let's suppose that there are people for whom the concept of forgiveness is decisive. They need it, as you said; they need it badly, even, obviously, on the basis of your experience. Did you not just say that?

Comment: I was saying that I did not feel the need for myself.

Dr. Tillich: No. No. What you said, I mean, now from your patients and so forth. Now you could tell these people -- a minister could tell them -- "Be assured. God has forgiven you. God is the God who forgives always." Of course, the presupposition is that you even want to be forgiven, that you feel there is something wrong, that something needs repentance, which means turning-on-one's-way.

Now lets see -- the people say, "Yes, we feel very badly. We want to be forgiven for this mistake we did to this other human being" -- for instance, hurting [that person] badly and so. Now one could ask, why is it not enough to receive this message, as we have it in the Old Testament, "if your sin is like blood, it will become like snow," so there is forgiveness. In the Psalms, of course, there is forgiveness with you, and so on. Why is that not enough? Why did Paul use the event of Golgatha in order to give a theological and/or a psychological addition to this, which has made it possible ever since for the Christians to be certain of the divine forgiveness?

The Anselmian Theory of Atonement

Here is my riddle. The theory say -- the Anselmian theological theory -- God could not forgive because [God] must exercise [God's] justice against the sin. The sin is infinite because it is directed against the infinite God. No human being can expiate for infinite guilt because [we are] finite. Only God Himself could do it. But [God] could not do it, since [God] cannot suffer in Himself. [God] could only suffer in a [human being]. And so, a [person] had to do it, and this [person] had to be divine. That is the whole theological construction.

Now this construction is very bad theory, I would say, and very good psychology' namely, good psychology in the sense that [Anselm] describes how people who are in despair again get assurance of forgiveness by the vision of the suffering God -- let's put it this way.

Dr. Johnson: I have a brainstorm, and I am going to break in. (Professor Tillich chuckles.) You know, earlier we were talking about the concept of self-love, which you have broken down into three things, one of which was self-acceptance. If a person accepts [oneself], does [one] need forgiveness?

Can a Person Forgive Oneself?

Dr. Tillich: The ideal is always the question. How can you accept yourself? This is the ultimate question. But then, the answer is: you cannot accept yourself, because you are guilty. You cannot say, "I am not guilty" if you feel guilty. No one can do this psychologically. Even in the psychoanalytic practice, you need somebody else who accepts you and takes you in and says, "Do not be worried. I am not a moralist. Lie down or sit down. We talk. I will see what you are. And let's forget about your guilt feeling." So there is acceptance by somebody.

Now I say, you cannot forgive yourself. Nobody will believe this act of forgiveness if [one] forgives [oneself]. The only way is to have a resource in the power of forgiveness which is in life, which can be called the divine power of forgiveness, to which you refer and of which you are aware and are perhaps certain. But it must be something which transcends not only the individual patient but also the analyst. Both the analyst and the patient are in the same boat of needing forgiveness and can get it only by being in relation to this that I call the power of forgiveness which is in life in order to get all mythological nonsense out of the way.

There is so much nonsense in theological language that I really want to talk psychologically so that it makes sense to me. If this mythological nonsense is all removed, then one thing remains. It is extremely hard to accept the fact that one is accepted, but that is the only way in which one can accept oneself. Now that is my whole statement.

Now the question is: how can you give certainty to somebody that [one] is accepted so that [one] can also accept [oneself]?

This certainty was given for a few thousand years, often, formerly, by the sacrificial cult where animals took the guilt away; and, then, finally, in the idea of the lamb of God who was slaughtered for our sins. This is the meaning of the cross in this kind of speech.

How is that psychologically understandable, please? I must confess that I have tried and tried to understand that. Theologically, I can see an answer, because in this image God Himself participates in our guilt; and, therefore, [God] is not the judge any more but the participant. This is perhaps a good theological answer.

Comment: Identification. People in our society feel so desperately guilty that they are able to expiate their sins through identification and the death on the cross.

Dr. Tillich: Identification with what?

Comment: With Christ.

Dr. Tillich: Now, yes, but with the crucified Christ, you mean? (Yes.)

Comment: Could we not admit the possibility that somewhere, let us say, one human being accepts another -- somehow, in some way, forgives [the person] or something? (Yes.) [One] experiences this other human being as a being forgiven?

Dr. Tillich: [That person] is also in need of forgiveness?

Comment: Yes. But somewhere along the line it might be possible -- because in a sense [that one] was forgiven -- [one] could forgive [oneself]. And ultimately, somehow, this thing of guilt just dissolves, so that this guilt experience is almost gone. I do not know if it is ever completely gone. Maybe for some people it might be -- a Buddha or someone like that.

Dr. Tillich: Now Buddha is another question because there this matter of guilt was never the predominant problem. There suffering was the predominant problem and guilt was not the central problem.

Is Guilt Universal?

Comment: This is what I am wondering about. Is there any other society at present in the whole world, or has there ever been, that feels as guilty as the Christian society does, that experiences such preoccupation with guilt?

Dr. Tillich: "Preoccupation" changes the question a little bit. Let's ask first whether guilt is there at all. There, I would say, it seems to be. Even in Mahayana Buddhism, we have it very strongly. It is not in Zen Buddhism, because Zen Buddhism is the self-force Buddhism or the self-power Buddhism, as it is called in unknown Japanese words or Indian words.[22] But Shin Buddhism is the outer-force -- the Amida Buddha.[23] Most of the statutes are Amida Buddha or Kwannon, the Goddess of Mercy, statues where mercy includes forgiveness, and these are functions of the Buddha spirit. The Buddha has (these functions) right and left -- wisdom and compassion. The divine compassion overcomes the individual guilt. So we have guilt in Buddhism also. He who calls the name of Amida in the right way -- in the right way is the big problem, of course -- will be taken up by Amida Buddha and relieved of the oppressive burden of worldly cares.

Dr. Johnson: I have an idea that I have never even tried out on myself. In some way guilt is a product of non-acceptance, I think. Guilt comes from failing to meet expectations.

In my mind, one of the major things is psychotherapy is a type of acceptance that does not -- maybe -- expect. I mean, it does not have a goal of what this person should be or do or feel but tries only to find the truth without expecting. By not having wants, the therapeutic relationship sets up an experience in which a person functions without an external demand. When [a person] can function this way, I think [one] comes to a type of acceptance that leads to a self-acceptance that frees from guilt.

* * *

Guilt and Guilt-Feelings

Dr. Tillich: In German, guilt means <u>schuld</u> and guilt-feeling means <u>schuldegefühl</u>. In English, the word guilt is used both for the fact and for the feeling. I know from many discussions that this creates a great confusion. Therefore, I always suggest that we consistently use guilt-feeling if we want to express the feeling of guilt, and guilt if we speak about somebody who commits a murder and is guilty now -- is under a guilt, stands under the judgment "You are guilty" in his conscience. There are two things. If [one] makes this clear distinction, then I would say, "Objectively, we always become guilty: namely, we always do things which we should not have done and do not things which we should have done." That is the famous formula of confession.

Now if that is the case, then the question is: what is the right reaction of our awareness to it? Shall we feel this as a tinge or as a pang of conscience, which is guilt feeling, or should we not? I would say, we should. We should because -- what gives us this uneasy feeling, which usually is called as uneasy conscience -- it is our essential being. We act against our essential being.

This brings me to your concept of expectancy. If we have what Karen Horney always liked to say is "the grandeur illusion" and then feel defeated if we do not get to this kind of perfection -- Christian theology has called it perfectionism -- then an unhealthy guilt-feeling develops. If you expect yourself to be Buddha or

Christ or even something better, then, of course, you must have continuous guilt-feelings because you did not reach it. Or even the grandeur in external things, if you have the idea of wanting to be a very successful business man and you always remain in a very mediocre position and this grandeur is really your ultimate concern, as I would call it, then, of course, guilt-feeling must develop.

But I think there is at the same time an essential guilt-feeling: namely, an expectation that we are what we essentially ought to be in a concrete situation. If this expectation, which is not a neurotic grandeur expectation, is not fulfilled, then the feeling of guilt is justified.

Comment: I think guilt is a normal or healthy emotion or feeling. Say a person does not live up to what [one] can see [oneself] clearly and actually to be. If [one] falls short of a realistic goal or does something that is opposed to [one's] own inner feelings, this I would consider to be guilt. But the thing that we see over and over is guilt-feelings that are completely unrelated and basic.

Comment: But are not the guilt-feelings actually masking the deeper guilt?

Dr. Johnson: That is the point, but I think what we have been calling guilt around here a lot may be really a feeling of guilt, which is a neurotic manifestation.

Dr. Tillich: I made the distinction in *The Courage to Be.* I mean, the reason I made the distinction is in order to save the real, the genuine guilt feeling, which is necessary in order to feel that there is in us an essential [humanity] and at the same time it is distorted by our actual existence. If this feeling is gone, then every impetus and every motive to ask the meaning of where is the genuine guilt has gone. Therefore, it is so important [to realize] that the idea that the analyst analyzes every guilt-feeling away reduces guilt. . . .

Comment: That is ridiculous.

Dr. Tillich: But this is produced. I think Karen Horney was very near to it.[24] She was a very near friend of mine, but we always had this discussion -- whether there is both a basic or existential guilt-feeling and anxiety and then a neurotic guilt-feeling and anxiety. She did not want to make this distinction. She wanted to liberate [people] as a kind of saviour -- not herself, but, I mean, her function -- from both of them together. Therefore, she did not really acknowledge the difference. She felt that every anxiety is neurotic and every guilt-feeling is neurotic.

Comment: I absolutely disagree. I want to ask you this question. Suppose, do you think it is possible, could a human being live guilt-less?

Dr. Tillich: Without objective guilt? No. No. How could [one] because we are all under the destiny of existential estrangement from our true being.

Comment: But this would be one of the things that would bring it about -- existential estrangement? (Yes.) Where this was not present, then there would not be guilt?

Dr. Tillich: There would be no life either because we would still be in what I like to call symbolically "dreaming innocence." I mean, before the self-actualization of life you can imagine a happy state of paradise, which is a mythological symbol for what Plato called the realm of pure essences. But that is not actual life.

In actual life -- with the self-realization of life in its individual character -- we always have estrangement from the essential reality at the same time. Therefore, guilt is something universal, because it goes through our freedom. Although it is universal, we know that we participate in this. It is, so to speak, a transcendent act in which every empirical act participates -- "so to speak" means, this is also symbolic. It is something which precedes every individual life. So there is universal guilt; there is universal guilt-feeling, in some way.

Now I did not analyze the stages of the "sitting" experience in the Zen Master before he becomes a Zen Master. How many lapses are there in him about which he has something of this guilt-feeling? "I should not have slept," for instance, which they always do and all these things. They do not call it guilt-feeling, but I think it is exactly the same thing.

I have seen deep guilt feeling in social relations among every Asiatic people, I mean, if they hurt the other one or they made a bad mistake. They had a tremendous guilt-feeling about this newspaper article in which I was called dead.[25] It was not their guilt; it was nobody's guilt; it was a misunderstanding at the phone about a Japanese word. But they had the feeling this man was guilty [the editor who had telephoned], and he must come and excuse himself. This kind of guilt is more social, then, perhaps, than in Christianity. It does not go as deep, but it is there. It cannot be denied.

* * *

Forgiveness and Acceptance

Dr. Tillich: Forgiveness is only the more vivid description of the more abstract term "being justified by grace through faith." Faith is receiving forgiveness; grace is the divine giving of forgiveness. The whole act is in a Paulinian terminology, which was a Rabbinic terminology, called justification. I do not use that term because nobody understands it today. It is simply only understandable if you have the Old Testament concept of tsedaqah[26] and so on. Therefore, I was looking for another term and replaced it by acceptance.

Comment: But to be declared right or justified and to have this experience is in a sense to be guiltless. (Yes.) Yet at the same time, though one is guiltless, one participates in brokenness; and despite brokenness, one is guiltless.

Dr. Tillich: Yes. Luther has formulated it most sharply: justus, in-justus; [whoever] is just is unjust. In this short formula he has put together the two things. Actually, somebody -- let us make the example the most external and objective example possible -- is a criminal, but he hears the word of forgiveness as symbolized in the man on the cross. For instance, one of the two criminals crucified with Jesus is accepted. This does not mean that he is not a criminal. He is guilty. But his guilt is taken up as forgiveness -- something which shall not be valid in the relationship of God and himself, as it is not valid in the relationship when we forgive each other: children, [person] and [person], man and wife, friends, and so on. This does not mean that we deny that there was something bad, but we accept the other one. Usually, we thank God, without a solemn act of forgiveness; we simply do it. But the other feels we disapprove; we are hurt, or so, nevertheless, we accept [the person].

Now this seems to be a good psychological analogy to the ultimate forgiveness.

* * *

The Uneasy Conscience

Dr. Tillich: God has saved us eternally. Yes, of course, but we must always become aware of this again if we fall into a kind of sin, if you want to call it -- I mean, sin as a concrete thing where we realize that we should not have done that -- we hurt somebody; we did something wrong; we were lazy or whatever it may be. It can go even farther; we had to lie, we lied, we betrayed -- all kinds of things which we always do. There, I would say, this produces a feeling of bad conscience. Let's avoid for a moment the world "guilt."

Now how do you overcome this feeling of uneasy conscience if it is very sharp, very hard, and gives you the feeling you are really separated in this moment from God or from the source of life or from the Ultimate or however you want to call it? What then?

Then, of course, the word of forgiveness has meant for innumerable people the overcoming of their uneasy conscience. They are accepted.

I think that the psychoanalyst in our period of history has largely had the function of the priest who made the statement -- "You are forgiven. You are accepted." [That person] accepts; [that one] takes them into community.

The church has become very mechanized about these things. On the other hand, the church has one thing beyond the analyst. The church also embraces the patient and the analyst. The analyst need the same thing that the patient needs. So there must be someplace from which this word of forgiveness must be told to somebody.

Now there may be people, I will not deny that, who tell it to themselves -- without self-betrayal, not in terms of self-complacency but in terms of a kind of meditative prayer, "Forgive us our sins as we forgive our debtors." All right. This is not said out loud; it is not a prayer; it is some inner meditative feeling, "In spite of this, I am in unity with God." But it is a very serious inner act, then. It is not, "I can take that easily."

Now, if it is not that easy act, then it is very similar to hearing the word of the minister or the word of the Bible or of the Church Fathers. Then the question comes -- we started this line of discussion with the question -- "What does the cross mean in this context?"

THE CROSS AND AMBIGUITY

I do not mean the cross which we see on the wall but the symbol of the cross itself. Why has the symbol had such an immense impact on the consciousness of people? -- I mean, for instance, a criminal who is executed is shown the cross. Why is that done? What is going on psychologically in this moment? Or in the child praying in the morning or evening -- better in the evening in this case --

"Forgive what I have done during the day" and looking at the cross? Or Thomas Aquinas, when he was dying and one of his friends (I do not know who it was, one of the other great theologians, Bonaventura, probably) tells him, "Now you did all this great theology and should not be worried about the salvation of your soul." And Aquinas said, "I have forgotten everything that I have ever written, but ..." and then he shows the cross of Christ, I mean, the crucifix.

* * *

Theological Shift in Western Christianity

Comment: To go back into history, is there something that happened in the fourth century as far as <u>kirchengeschichte</u>[27] is concerned -- did the philosophy in the Church change at that time? I am very curious to find out.

Dr. Tillich: Not the official theology too much, because the Greek theology was taken over by the Roman Western part of Christianity. But there was a great change in emphasis. The Greek ontological thinking was officially accepted. I mean, the dogmas were finished, practically in the fifth but officially in the seventh century. They were taken over.

Then, when the Western world developed independently, some motives -- you must call them motives of thought -- became emphasized which were already in the Bible and in the early church, for instance, the humility of Christ. In the Greek mosaics -- Greek Orthodox mosaics in all these wonderful Ravennine churches[28] and so on -- you always have Christ Pantocrator, which means the World Ruler,[29] with these majestic forms of the mosaics. You never have him crucified;[30] but in the Romanesque period,[31] you have these extremely realistic crucifixes, which are like expressionistic forms of the twentieth century.[32]

Comment: Do you detect an element of masochism?

Dr. Tillich: Yes, that might be. On the other hand, instead of the ontological hierarchy with Christ on the top, it also meant the active and dynamic participation of God in the life of the lowest in a new way. Therefore, it has to do with the human character of Christ, which was more or less lost in the Eastern Church and still is by the Monophysitic development.[33] There is only one nature -- the divine; the human nature of Christ is lost. This is anhypothetic,[34] as it is called in a terrible scholastic term. It has no hypostasis -- that is, one's own substantia; it is in the substantia of the divine.

Now this terrible formula means something very realistic. It meant that the human image of Jesus became completely lost in the Eastern Church. That human image came out again in the Western Church, partly under Augustine's influence. It was the reason for the emphasis upon the crucifixion pictures, which now came up, and also the feeling of sin and guilt. The problem of justification, in the Pauline way, came up again.

The interesting thing is that Paul was almost eliminated in the Eastern Church very shortly after the New Testament period. Instead of that, there was always the Fourth Gospel (John), which decided the [thought of the] Eastern Church. There the problems of eternal life and life -- knowledge and light -- are decisive. That is quite different from Paul where from the rabbinic tradition the problem is guilt -- fulfillment of the law and the inability to do it. That other side came up again in the Western World. Paul was rediscovered in the West.

Therefore, we have different periods of Paulinism. Augustine was Paulinian. Thomas Aquinas had strongly Paulinian elements. Then, the Reformation was a revolt of Paulinism against the whole Roman Church. This meant the symbol for the cross was the central symbol.

Comment: Somehow they needed this. Maybe the two were necessary -- interrelated -- guilt, forgiveness, the cross.

What Can Symbolize Forgiveness?

Dr. Tillich: Yes, good. But we have not yet fully answered her question, perhaps nobody can: Why the psychological power of this symbol? The question which is most important for me is whether this same psychological power can be produced by mediative self-acceptance without the relationship to the symbol of the cross?

Comment: I think so.

Dr. Tillich: You think so?

Comment: It seems like a very different experience for me. They are the same in many ways, but I think that the miraculous -- really sort of large miracle, I don't know how to say it -- quality that is related to the symbol of the cross is very different. It is not really the same without it. I am trying to think what this symbol would be where the experience of telling it to oneself was present and I do not know what it would be.

Dr. Tillich: Of forgiving oneself?

Comment: Yes.

Dr. Tillich: We were clear about that earlier in our discussion. We cannot do it simply and directly. We can do it through the power of forgiveness, because life has forgiven us or has accepted us. Only if this [forgiveness] is in the meditative element, only then, can it be done. Otherwise, it is simply saying, "I am a good [person]," but that is just the opposite of what forgiveness means.

So the question is: What is the symbol of forgiveness in the ground of being itself or in the power of life itself if it is not the cross? I try in my theology to reinterpret the cross in this sense so that one does not need to make [one's] assurance dependent upon the event, as a sacrificial, substitutionary suffering and this whole Anselmian idea. I think this is really almost impossible for us today.

You have much more experience with people, but I think it is impossible.

Can The Cross Be Reinterpreted?

So, what can we say? Now I say what is right theologically, I mean, what can be found in Paul is that God is reconciled by the death of Christ as the sacrificial substitute. But God is everything; [God] does it; and [God] shows it. Now how does [God] show it if not in this way? That was the last question asked. Is there another symbol? you said. Can the symbol of the cross be reinterpreted? Can it get another meaning? Or is this impossible?

Comment: This may be absolute nonsense, but it seems to me that in the cross the symbol is somehow focusing on something. But where the cross is gone, somehow this experience, then, is pervasive; and in some way it is almost trans-symbolic.

Dr. Tillich: Yes. All right. Let's forget now about the three level symbol: the cross on the wall; the event, the cross of a man Jesus, who was the Christ; and then, the original meaning, namely, God's acceptance of estranged [humanity]. All right, these are the three levels of the symbol.

Now can this be expressed in the same convincing way as that which really produces, which has produced, which still produces in innumerable people, the conquest of their uneasy conscience? Can we have another symbol for it or, at least, another experience? Perhaps we are not able to have a symbol for it today; but if we can have this experience, I would be greatly relieved because I know how infinitely difficult it is to understand all these terrible associations -- what you called, the whole scene of miracles around it. We must get rid of all this, of course. How is it possible?

Dr. Johnson: You gave me a prod. I may be clear out in left field, but it is with me. You mentioned that the flow is, in a sense, back and forth between God and [humanity]. If you put a piece across it, in some way could it symbolize the difficulty or the barrier in our communication?

Dr. Tillich: Yes. But it has the idea in Christianity of opening up the communication.

Dr. Johnson: But I mean, it cannot open up something, I mean, opening is only important when there is a closure.

Dr. Tillich: Yes. The closure is that we are driven out of paradise. That is the Biblical symbol. We are not in "dreaming innocence," which sometimes is wrongly identified with childhood.

* * *

Dr. Johnson: Does this symbol crop up in people who are aware or people who are relatively unaware [of the barrier and difficulty of communicating with God]?

Comment: Sometimes my patients seem to develop this, no question about it.

Dr. Johnson: I know; mine do not; and that is why I am kind of curious.

Comment: In one man patient of mine it is evident that this is a real symbol of rebirth and redemption and that he lost himself some place. This experience is really shaking. My hair was rising on the back of my head as this thing came up in therapy. I knew I was in the presence of the numinous.

Dr. Tillich: To which point do you refer the word "this?" The cross you mean?

Comment: The cross, yes. He came to this, you see ...

Dr. Tillich: Oh yes. Now that is what you can find in churches all the time and in dying people, for instance. It is really the consolation.

We are now in a situation where many of us would prefer that we had another symbol or no symbol at all, perhaps, simply the description of the experience in our inner acceptance that we are accepted without having this addition, which is often mostly in Christian prayers, "Because of the innocent suffering and dying of thy son Jesus Christ." That is the last sentence of all the official prayers for forgiveness.

Now I must confess this "because" has no sense for me. I would say, "as it is manifest." That would be my formulation of the prayer. So, in this sense it would be a symbol for me.

Now if this is not even possible any more -- I mean, this "as it is manifest" formula -- then this symbol is gone. Then, is there another symbol?

Comment: What I think it is -- and I can only say how it seems to me -- is that it is like the Zen. The Zen idea seems to be helpful to me -- the Zen idea of a gateless gate. When you are there, you see the gate. Once you go through, you realize there was no gate in the first place. Maybe, in the same way the cross is necessary, and after this, somehow, it becomes transparent; and it is gone. Somehow it is so paradoxical.

Dr. Tillich: Yes. Now, of course, in Christian symbolism what you say can be understood, then, as only the resurrection is left --the resurrection, again, not in the miraculous absurdity but in the sense that out of this death, life is born. That you can say. There is a double step. In classical Christian theology (in the Bible and the New Testament) there is never the cross alone. There is always the cross and resurrection. There is never the resurrection alone. It is always the resurrection of the crucified. These two belong to each other, absolutely.

This is a very important discussion for me, because I really see how difficult it is -- even to reinterpret the symbol in this modified form "as manifest" instead of "because of." If this is gone, there is not other symbol. All these other symbols such as Zen Buddhism has are very highly unhistorical symbols.

Comment: We have to stop in about five minutes

Dr. Tillich: Oh, I am sorry we have to stop. This is a wonderful discussion.

* * *

The Deepest Problem

Dr. Tillich: I would still emphasize the problem of guilt more than anything else. I am glad, for instance, that Karen Horney (and other psychoanalytic friends) have informed me that with these enlightened people of New York, Park Avenue, and so on, who were her patients, there is always a point where she comes down to the problem of guilt. Although one thinks they are so humanistic and naturalistic, that this problem would not mean anything, it is not true. I do not know what you feel about that fact. It is an astonishing fact. But it is a fact that the problem of guilt, in spite of the problem of death and the problem of meaning, which are three main problems -- although the problem of meaning is, perhaps, externally the most conspicuous today -- in the depths of everybody, the problem of guilt plays a tremendous role.

Therefore, I think we should not make it too easy for them in swallowing the problem of acceptance. They must come into community with objective transpersonal powers of forgiveness or of acceptance in order to be able to accept themselves. Otherwise, it is simply a self-confirmation in a state of estrangement.[35]

Comment: Well, if we are not aware of this, if we go in blindness ourselves, all we do is give people a handy set of rationalizations so they can still get away from really dealing with this fundamental difficulty.

Dr. Tillich: Yes. Yes. They can go on. I think it is a danger in some groups of psychologists, perhaps the more orthodox Freudians, that there the difference between essence and existence is not made. Therefore, there is no judgment from essence against existence. Therefore, anxiety can be analyzed away; guilt feelings can be analyzed away. I think this is the point where the Christian tradition is profounder.

Dr. Johnson: I just realized that I had been by-passing guilt. I mean, I have gone from where we are trying to help a person become inner-directed and self-supporting so that the problem of guilt does not actually come up in therapy, except as it is expressed as a feeling. I think I will spend some time going into that.

* * *

FOOTNOTES

1.   The conversation took place on the back porch of Richard L. Johnson, M.D., then Director of the psychiatric residency program and the Out-patient Clinic at the State Hospital in Columbus, Ohio. Also present were: James B. Ashbrook, B.D.; Elizabeth Barker, Ph.D.; Rahe Corlis, Ph.D.; Jane Gavins, M.S.W.; Harvey Guthrie, B.D.; Rosanna Koch, M.D.; Benjamin Kovitz, M.D.; and Vincent O'Connell, Ph.D. Dr. Tillich understood he was simply to be "present" in an informal give-and-take on issue growing of psychotherapeutic experience. "Paul Tillich Converses with Psychotherapists" originally appeared in *Journal of Religion and Health,* Vol. 11, Number 1, January, 1972, pp. 40-72, in a slightly different form. Some footnotes have been updated and inclusive language added.

2.   Professor Tillich visited Japan in May, June and July 1960, at the invitation of Professor Yasaka Takagi, to whom he dedicated his book, *Christianity and the Encounter of the World Religions.* See

Wilhem & Marion Pauck, *Paul Tillich: His Life & Thought Volume I: Life* (New York: Harper & Row, 1976, pp. 245-261) for a description of the visit.

3.   Zen Buddhism is one of the principal sects (shu) of Buddhism in Japan. It disavows abstraction, generalization, explanation, argument. Instead it appeals directly to facts of personal experience without any intermediary. Zen literature is extensive. A sample includes: Philip Kapleau, *The Three Pillars of Zen: Teaching, Practice, Enlightenment.* Forward by Huston Smith. Boston: Beacon Press, 1967; Daisetz T. Suzuki, *Essays in Zen Buddhism.* First Series. New York: Grove Press, 1961; R. H. Blyth, *Zen and Zen Classics,* Vols. I, I, VII. Tokyo: The Hokuseido Press, 1960-64; selected articles in *The Eastern Buddhist (New Series)* published by The Eastern Buddhist Society, Otani University, Kyoto, Japan.

4.   The True Pure Land Sect or Jodo - Shin - Shu. Its founder claimed that the sect "truly" transmits the faith and thought of the Pure Land Sect. (D. T. Suzuki, *Zen and Japanese Buddhism.* Rutland, VT: Charles E. Tuttle Company, 1958, p. 109) The True Pure Land Sect is based upon the 18th vow: "Having heard the name of Amida, they rejoice and trust in him with the whole heart." This vow is the most liberal of Buddhist vows and because of its popular interpretation may account, in part, for the success of the sect.

5.   "In the dialogue between Christianity and Buddhism two telos [the intrinsic aim of existence] formulas can be used: in Christianity the telos of everyone and everything united in the Kingdom of God; in Buddhism the telos of everything and everyone fulfilled in the Nirvana." (Paul Tillich, *Christianity and the Encounter with the World Religions,* New York: Columbia University Press, 1963, p. 64) See Masao Abe, "Review Article: Christianity and the Encounter of the World Religions." *The Eastern Buddhist* Vol. 1, No. 1 (New Series) September 1965, pp. 109-122, for a critically sympathetic analysis and interpretation of the differences between Christianity and Buddhism as presented by Tillich.

6.   "The Zen master would say, 'My words are mine and not yours and do not belong to you. All must come out of your own being.'" To avid abstract metaphysical speculations that detract one from the concrete world of finites, the Zen master makes illogical retorts to the question in order to jolt the student into seeing for oneself. This characteristic feature of question and answer is called mondo. The mondo have a freshness and vivacity "because they spring from life and deal with it directly without any intermediary agent such as intellection or symbolization." (*Encyclopedia Britannica,* Vol. 23. Chicago: University of Chicago Press, 1962) Also see D. T. Suzuki, Erich Fromm, and Richard DeMartino, *Zen Buddhism and Psychoanalysis.* New York: Grove Press, 1960, pp. 24-32, 142-171 ("The Human Situation and Zen Buddhism.") Zen koans are problems posed by a master to a pupil which cannot be solved by the intellect. The largest collection in English of classical and modern koans, with commentary, is Gyomay M. Kubose, *Zen Koans.* Original sumi illustrations by Ryozo Ogura. Chicago: Henry Regnery Company, 1973.

7.   Technically, "to sit" means to sit cross-legged in mediation. It refers to a motionless sitting and some sort of concentrating or peaceful attention to the object without straining to achieve effects. Usually the legs are crossed, the back straight, the breathing regular, and the eyes only slightly open. (Ernest Wood, *Zen Dictionary.* New York: Philosophical Library, 1962, p. 157)

8.   D. T. Suzuki, 1870 - 1966 lived in New York City from 1951 on most of the time. See "In Memoriam: Daisetz Teitaro Suzuki," *The Eastern Buddhist,* Vol. II, NA. 1 (New Series) August 1967.

9.   Shin'ichi Hisamatsu. (See Suzuki, Fromm, and DeMartino, op. cit., 1960, p. 142.) He was former Professor of Buddhism, Kyoto University and Director of F.A.S. Zen Institute. They held three discussions when Professor Hisamatsu was visiting Professor at the Harvard Divinity School. Dr. Hisamatsu Shin'ichi (Part One), *The Eastern Buddhist,* Vol. IV, No. 2 (New Series) October 1971, pp. 89-107; (Part Two), Vol. V, No. 2 (New Series) October

1972, pp. 107-128; (Part Three), Vol. VI, No. 2 (New Series) October 1973, pp. 87-114). Masao Abe and Richard DeMartino are gathering Dr. Hisamatsu's writings for publication.

10. According to legend, Buddhism was thought to have originated in India and was then taken to China in finished form by Bodhidharma early in the 6th century A.D. The actual origin in China began with the 6th century patriarch Hui-neong (died 713 A.D.). He emphasized prajna, which is essential wisdom that transcends the subject-object dualism, in contract to the"one-sided mental absorption in the tranquilizing practice of dhyana meditation or contemplation of union with Reality that was the prevailing tendency in his day." (*Encyclopedia Britannica,* op. cit.)

The change and adaptation that took place are seen in the establishment of such schools of Buddhism as those which developed skills in "classification by chronological periods and compromise between Indian metaphysics and Chinese worldly thought"; emphasized faith and the doctrine of abrupt Enlightenment as "the outcome of the Chinese bent for simplicity, directness, and practicality"; emphasized filial piety; and developed the close liaison with the imperial government. (K.K.S. Ch'en, *Buddhism in China*: a historical survey. Princeton, NJ: Princeton University Press, 1964, pp. 484-486.

11. Either in 538 or 552 A.D., one of the Korean Kings presented a Buddhist image to the Japanese court, along with copies of Buddhist scriptures and liturgical ornaments. Although Buddhism had been known earlier among Japanese of Chinese and Korean ancestry, these are the dates usually regarded as the beginning of Buddhism in Japan. (Kenneth W. Morgan, Ed., *The Path of The Buddha*: Buddhism interpreted by Buddhists. New York: Ronald Press, 1964, pp. 64-65, 307-363, "Buddhism in Japan")

12. Professor Tillich dedicated his book, *Theology of Culture,* to "Hanna and Gerhard Colm." Hanna Colm was in Berlin from 1923-1927 as lecturer in Child Guidance at the School for Social

Work of Dr. Alice Salomon, and Pestalozzi-Frobel-Haus. Professor Tillich was <u>Privatdozent</u> of Theology at the University of Berlin form 1919-1924.

13.   The Japanese word for "sitting" is <u>za-zen</u>. Also see footnote 7.

14.   In those discussions (see note 9), translator Richard DeMartino kept hoping that Dr. Hisamatsu would give Tillich something "akin to a poke in the stomach" as a "blockbusting non-verbal" response to Tillich's inquiry about Hisamatsu's "'existential presentation' through the use of concepts." ("Dialogues, East and West," *The Eastern Buddhist* (Part Three), Vol. VI, No. 2, October 1973, p. 114) Enlightenment is apparently a constantly experienced state of <u>satori</u> or getting beyond concepts. It is an added mode of experience similar to the opening of a third eye. "<u>Satori</u> may be defined as an intuitive looking into the nature of things in contradistinction to the analytical or logical understanding of it. Practically, it means the unfolding of a new world hitherto unperceived in the confusion of a dualistically-trained mind." (D. T. Suzuki, *Zen Buddhism*; selected writings. Edited by William Barrett. Garden City, New York: Doubleday Anchor Books, 1956, pp. 83-108).

15.   The Shingon-shū was brought to Japan by Kobo Dishi from China in 806 A.D. It is one of the most powerful and prosperous Buddhist sects in Japan. The sect regards its own teachings as "secret or esoteric doctrine" and all other Buddhist teachings as "open or exoteric doctrine." (Robert C. Armstrong, *An Introduction to Japanese Buddhist Sects.* Canada: Privately printed by Mrs. Robert Cornell Armstrong, 1950, pp, 166-197)

16.   As a religion, Buddhism has given the world two major values: (1) "the idea of personal discipline to gain freedom from craving in the ultimate tranquility in Nirvāna"; and (2) "the idea of unselfish devotion to the good of others for the sake of their deliverance from ill." (Clarence H. Hamilton, *Buddhism: A*

Religion of Infinite Compassion: Selections from Buddhist Literature. Edited, with an Introduction and Notes. New York: The Liberal Arts Press, 1952, p. xxiii) The second of the four states in cultivating the unlimited emotions is compassion. It requires concentrating on the suffering of others in order to suffer with them, and thereby desire to remove their suffering. With Mahayanists, compassion achieved a rank of importance equal with wisdom. (Edward Donze, *Buddhism: Its Essence and Development.* Oxford, England: Bruno Cassirer, 1957, pp. 102, 128)

17.   "In the traditional terminology of Buddhism, self-nature is Buddhanature, that which makes up Buddahood; it is absolute Emptiness, Sunyata, it is absolute Suchness, Tathata . . . it has nothing to yet with a dualistic world of subject and object. . . ." (Suzuki, *Zen Buddhism*, op. cit., 1956, pp. 210-211, 220.)

18.   Etienne Gilson interprets Augustine on love: "The moral problem is not whether one should love but what one should love. 'Are you told not to love anything? Not at all! If you are to love nothing, you will be lifeless, dead, detestable, miserable. Love, but be careful what you love.' Virtue, then, means to will what we should will, i.e., to love what we should love." (*The Christian Philosophy of Saint Augustine,* translated by L. E. M. Lynch. New York: Random House, 1960, p. 135)

19.   Anselm's theory of atonement "starts with the tension in God between [God's] wrath and [God's] love and shows that the work of Christ makes it possible for God to exercise mercy without violating the demands of justice. . . . Only the God-[Human] could do this, because as [human], [God] could suffer and, as God, [God] did not have to suffer for [God's] own sins." (Paul Tillich, *Systematic Theology,* Vol. II, Chicago: University of Chicago Press, 1957, pp. 172-173)

20.   From the late Constantinian period "the death of Christ is alluded to by other scenes, but is never actually portrayed. . . . The cross of Golgatha served as a symbol of the crucifixion, as on a sar-

cophagus in the Lateran Museums." (Wolfgang F. Volbach, *Early Christian Art.* New York: Harry N. Abrams, Photography by Max Hirmer, n.d., p. 22) A more or less historically conceived crucifixion is "seldom found in the 5th century and the definitive composition originates in the 6th, perhaps in Jerusalem. The 5th century efforts are shapeless and distasteful; it is only later that a worthy form is achieved." (F. vander Meer and Christine Mohrmann, *Atlas of the Early Christian World.* Translated and edited by Mary F. Hedlund and H. H. Rowley. New York: Nelson, 1958, p. 145)

21. In a Radio/Television conversation with Carl Rogers he described his view of the necessity of translating and interpreting the symbols of faith instead of replacing them: "I don't believe that scientific language is able to express the vertical dimension adequately, because it is bound to the relationship of finite things to each other, even in psychology and certainly the physical sciences. This is the reason why I think we need another language, and this language is the language of symbols and myths; it is religious language. But we poor theologians, in contrast to you happy psychologists, are in the bad situation that we know the symbols with which we deal have to be reinterpreted and even radically reinterpreted. But I have taken this heavy yoke upon myself and I have decided long ago I will continue to the end with it." (*Paul Tillich and Carl Rogers - a dialogue.* Produced and directed by T. D. Skinner; edited by R. E. Lee. Radio/Television, San Diego State College, and the Western Behavioral Sciences Institute, La Jolla, California, January, 1966)

22. Zen Buddhism is par excellence the religion of self-power by virtue of the fact one attempts to achieve Enlightenment by one's own efforts of study and ascetic practice. The Japanese word for self-effort is jiriki. (Christmas Humphreys, *Buddhism.* Middlesex, England: Penguin Books, 1949, p. 170)

23. In contrast to jiriki or self-power of Zen is tariki or otherpower of Jodo Shin. It expresses the idea of salvation by faith in

Another's Power. Shin is the Pure Land School of Buddhism in Japan in its extreme form of salvation by pure faith, the doctrine that [a human being] may be born in paradise simply by repeating the name of Amida Buddha. (Armstrong, op. cit., pp. 211-217)

24.   See Karen Horney, *New Ways in Psychoanalysis.* New York: Norton, 1939, pp. 237-238.

25.   See Hannah Tillich, *From Time to Time* (New York: Stein and Day, 1973, p. 214) for a description of the circumstances of the embarrassment which resulted from a misspelling as a result of his having drunk too much saki the evening previously.

26.   Tsedaqah or "righteousness." In the Old Testament it implies conforming to the norm of the character of God -- an ethical idea that was linked with salvation. (Alan Richardson, Ed., *A Theological Word Book of the Bible.* New York: Macmillan, 1951, pp. 202-204) Paul means by the righteousness of God the salvation which God accomplishes through Christ (Romans 3:21-26).

27.   German for church history.

28.   Professor Tillich's second wife, Hannah Werner, was an art student.   After their marriage in March, 1924, they went on a three-month walking tour through Italy where she introduced him to the fascinating wonders of Medieval and Renaissance painting and architecture. "For years afterwards," he said, "I dreamed of the 24 hours we spent in Ravenna." (*Time*, March 16, 1959, pp. 47-48.) "What no amount of study of church history had brought," he is reported to have said, "was accomplished by the mosaics in ancient Roman basilicas." (James Luther Adams, *Paul Tillich's Philosophy of Culture, Science, and Religion.* New York: Harper & Row, 1965, p. 66.) Also see Pauck, op. cit., p. 97; H. Tillich, op. cit., p. 118.

29.   "Byzantine art represented the Christ of all time, the Alpha and Omega, the beginning and the end. The CEFALU CHRIST has the mystery of the creator of the universe and the power of him who, in the words of the Te Deum Laudamas, we believe 'shalt

come to be our judge.'" The majestic, divine, and transcendent Christ was often of tremendous size. In some mosaics the head of Christ alone is about eight feet in height. Its placement on a concave area above the altar gives the image an impression that is overwhelming. (Jane Dillenberger, *Style and Content in Christian Art.* Nashville: Abingdon, 1965, pp. 59, 52)

30. For example, in Sant' Apollinere Nuovo are Passion scenes on the top zone of the south side of the three-aisled basilica: "The Last Supper, Christ in Gethsemane, The Kiss of Judas, Christ Led to Caiaphas, Christ Before Caiaphas, Christ Foretelling the Denial of Peter, The Denial of Peter, the Repentance of Judas, Christ Before Pilate, The Road to Calvary, the Marys at the Sepulcher, The Road to Emmaus, and The Incredulity of Thomas" (Wolfgang F. Volbach, op. cit., p. 341), but there is no scene of the crucifixion itself.

31. In the West, the Romanesque period was a time of upheaval with the invasions of Northern barbarian tribes and the weakening of the political, social, and economic structure. Varying degrees of classical, barbarian and Byzantine elements are welded together in an emerging style. "Byzantine art presents groups of figures as so many isolated beings near each other but with no relationship to each other beyond that of gesture. In Romanesque art the groups are bound by intense emotional reaction to the event." "The Christ of Romanesque art is either the dominant and transcendent presence in a scene as THE PENTECOST; or the Christ of the Apocalypse seen in glory in heaven and surrounded by the symbols of the four evangelists; or the Christ who as judge rules over the separation of the elect from the damned at the Last Judgment. All of these subjects are supernatural subjects of visionary and mystical elements" in a nonnaturalistic style (Dillenberger, op. cit., pp. 57-65.)

Western Christianity emphasized Christ's historical humanity, his humility, while Eastern Christianity emphasized his divinity, his victory.

32. In Romanesque art, the artist distorts the human figure in order to convey an emotion or idea, thus the style may be called expressionistic.

33. Monos means "one"; physis means "nature." Monophysitism insisted that "the human character of Christ was swallowed up in divinity. . . ." The East reacted against the Chalcedonian formula of the full humanity of Christ "to such a degree that it became an easy prey to the Islamic puritan reaction . . . against the sacramental superstitious forms into which Christianity had fallen more and more. I have a thesis . . . that the attacks of Islam would never have been successful if Eastern Christianity had taken into itself the element of personality and history." (*Tillich, A History of Christian Thought.* Edited by Carl E. Braaten, London: SCM Press, 1968, pp. 81, 87-88.)

34. Hypostatis means "being an independent being." Leontius of Byzantius in the 6th century stated that "the human nature in Christ does not have its own hypostasis; it is anhypostatis (without hypostasis). . . . When it comes to the formula enhypostasis [one hypostatis in the other], we do not really know what that means. But the reason it was invented is clear. The question was: Can two natures exist without an independent head; an hypostasis? The answer was, they cannot. Therefore, Christ has one hypostasis representing the two natures. . . . The two natures are distinguished only in theory, not in practice. The person of the Logos has become the personal center of a man. The human nature has no personal characteristics of its own. This was the decisive point, because if this is the case, how can He help us? The Crucified is the true God and Lord of glory, and one of the Trinity. The identification of Jesus Christ with the Logos is complete. As in the icons in which Christ appears in gold-ground setting, the human personality has disappeared. (*A History of Christian Thought, op. cit.,* pp. 88-89.)

35. In a memorial tribute to Professor Tillich, psychoanalyst Erik H. Erikson spoke of Tillich's "reiterated . . . concern about the

faddish aspects of psychoanalysis. Instead of restricting itself to removing neurotic self-contradictions so as to free in [people] what he called 'the moral self-realization of the centered self,' did not attempt to remove [a person's] existential dread along with [one's] neurotic anxiety? And what was [a person] without the awareness of [one's] finitude, what without the realization of [one's] guilt in regard 'to acts of which,' as he put it elsewhere, 'responsibility cannot be denied, in spite of the elements of destiny in them?' . . . Paulus acknowledge Freud's basic discoveries as having shown up 'the ambiguity of what he called [people] of good will . . . so rampant in . . . Protestantism.'" (*Harvard Divinity Bulletin,* January 1966, 30, 20, p. 15)

CULTURE AND RELIGION[1]

Dr. Tillich: I am very grateful to you who have planned this gathering that I do not need to make one more speech. I have to make too many speeches. I think sometimes the old Platonic dialogue is much more fruitful than anything else.[2]

THE RELATION OF CULTURE AND RELIGION

Question: I have difficulty understanding a statement you made, Professor Tillich, which says that religion is the substance of culture and culture is the form of religion. Could you explain what you mean by this statement?

Dr. Tillich: When you ask this question, I am tempted to act against my own preference for dialogue, and I suppose your preference, and make a speech because your question is the most embracing question which I think could be asked. Several years ago in Yale University I had to speak about religion and culture. I said I will do it in such a way that I make this statement the text and everything I say is the commentary. And the commentary lasted at least one hour and a quarter (laughter). So, it is not so easy for me to answer that question briefly, but I prefer to do it briefly because I want other questions and other criticisms to come up.

Substance and Form

Now in this statement, which you ask about, substance means the meaning-giving power. I do not use the word spiritual foundation. You can use that, too, but the word spiritual is ambiguous. That is true whether it is written with a capital S or a small s,[3] so I do not use it much. The other idea is that culture is the form of religion. That means every meaning-given idea or interpretation of human existence must express itself in special forms. These forms are theoretical forms and practical forms. They include ethics, aesthetics, the artistic side, the cognitive side, the theological systems, the political side, and the organization of the church. All this is taken out of the culture process.

Now these two sides influence each other, of course. The leading interpretation of life or the leading idea influences culture which, in exchange, gives forms for the expression of this idea. On the other hand, the forms influence the expression of the leading idea and therefore have influence on its character. So this is a mutual interrelationship of a very strict character.

Preservation of Ultimacy

Now let me say that after this general definition why this is important. This is important because it saves religion from the position into which is has often been pushed, which I call the corner position of emotional self-relatedness without real relevance for the other sides of culture. This, of course, is a situation which is not worthy of religion. It loses its real meaning, which I define, as probably most of you know, as ultimate concern. Religion is the state of being ultimately concerned.

An ultimate concern cannot be a particular concern besides other concern. I may express this in an expression of a hate I have. The word which I hate most in the English language and which I think is the most blasphemous word is "religionist." "Religionist" means making religion a special function of some people and then putting it aside and leaving it there in the hands of these funny people who are called "religionists." Now against any such distortion the idea that religion is the substance of culture -- that which gives it its inexhaustible and ultimate meaning -- is a protection. If this is the case, then, of course, religion in this large sense of the word cannot be a corner reality. It is something which is in the depths of everything.

Of course, there is, on the other hand, the actualized religion -- the religion which needs forms, the religion which must express itself. We cannot express an ultimate concern without expressing it in concrete symbols of action and thinking. That is what the concrete religion does. It receives for this purpose its forms of thought (philosophy, for instance) or of artistic style (for instance, the styles in the Christian churches and in Christian art through the centuries and millennia) or of the ethical principles and rules or of the political relations (the whole society and its relations) from the culture. All of this goes into the actual church and makes actual religion dependent upon the given culture. Now I think this is a preliminary answer, which shortens the one hour and twenty minutes.

WHAT IS A CHRISTIAN CULTURE?

Question: Dr. Tillich, would you expand on what you would mean by a Christian culture? Has there ever been a Christian culture, and if so, how would this be characterized as different from any other religious culture?

Dr. Tillich: This also is a very difficult question, but it is partly answered in what I said to the first question. A Christian culture would be a culture which is influenced by the concrete symbols in which the Christian church expresses its ultimate concern.

For instance, a discussion which I had in the first conversation brings me to this idea.[4] The way in which the Eastern church in the first thousand years (and beyond that) interpreted the message of Jesus as the Christ -- the Christian message -- largely determined the character of the Byzantine art[5] from the catacombs to San Marco in Venice.[6] This [cultural] development belongs definitively to the Christian development. It could not have been developed in the same way on any other soil than on the soil of the Christian church.

Visual Art in Japan

In May, June and July, I was in Japan. I saw the influence of Buddhist art through the centuries in Japan and in the Chinese predecessors, from which Japanese Buddhism and its art come. There you can see how the different ultimate concerns of the Buddhists, on the one hand, and of the Christian church, on the other, have produced fundamentally different expressions in the realm of the visual art.[7]

Philosophy in Greece

I could go to philosophy as another example. Neoplatonism was the great synthesis of the oriental mystical elements of Hellenism and of the classical Greek form of thought.[8] After Christianity conquered Neoplatonism, philosophy slowly developed, no longer on the basis of Apollo and Dionysus but, on the basis of Yahweh and the Christ, of Judaism and Christianity. The influence of this is very clear in the Renaissance. One of the most interesting inquiries is to see how all the great Greek philosophical schools were renewed -- Platonism, Aristotelianism, Pythagorianism, Stoicism, Epicureanism, Neoplatonism, and so on. All of them in their innermost character were somehow transformed. They got what I would call a Christian underground.

I could prove this transformation by showing, for instance, the influence of the non-Greek idea of creation.[9] This is not a story of "once upon a time" but is a present day valuation for all of us as creaturely or finite beings. Now this idea has influenced the reception by the Greek culture from the Christian underground so that something other than the classical Greek idea came out of all these schools. I cannot go into this now, but this would be an example of what I would call a Christian culture in the realm of the arts and of philosophy. But I could go on and on with other examples.

The High Middle Ages

Question: Would the high Middle Ages be such a culture, Dr. Tillich?

Dr. Tillich: Now the high Middle Ages was, of course, a Christian culture. It was prepared by that development which I just described. It was at first very much the Byzantine influence initially and beyond this. Then slowly the independent Romanist influence developed, and some Germanic elements came. Here again we can see how the elements of the Germanic tribes, the old Saxon art and all this, have been transformed under their influence of the basic Christian ideas.

I can give another example in the Middle Ages. It is the social structure, which was probably also in your mind when you asked that question. The social structure was Christian culture. It was, of course, feudal order and feudal order did exist before. But this feudal order was transformed by the fact that the substance of the life of the Germanic-Romanic tribes, when they became nations and united under the Pope and the Emperor, became the church. All cultural life, all educational life, all philosophy was given to this society by what the church had saved out of its own past and also out of the past of the ancient world generally. So we can say that this was a Christian culture.

We should be careful, however, to avoid one mistake. If we use the word "Christian" culture and think of a culture in which everybody is a Christian or in which the structures of society are determined by the Sermon on the Mount, then, of course, the concept becomes absurd. In this sense there never was and never will be a Christian culture. The Christian culture is described in the last book of the Bible as the heavenly Jerusalem, and we are not in it yet (laughter).

CHRISTIANITY AND ART

Question: Dr. Tillich, in your book *Theology of Culture* you make a statement to the effect that of all the styles of the history of Protestantism the twentieth century style in visual arts is best able to express the human condition as Christianity sees it. Could you elaborate on this in view of the fact that Symbols have become personal and that art in general today is non-figurative and makes no reference to the real world?

The Existential Style

Dr. Tillich: Ohhh (laughter). A series of lectures (more laughter). First I stick to my guns. (laughter) I believe, indeed, that the visual arts (as well as the other arts) which have developed since about 1900 are the dominant style of the twentieth century.[10] That is a very vague number, but somehow in the visual arts it is not so vague because that was the year in which the influence of Cezanne[11] began to be important. In any case, there were predecessors of this style at the end of the nineteenth century in drama, poetry, music and so on. In any case, there we now have this style.

Now I call this style, which has developed definitely and clearly in all realms of life, by the term "the existentialist style." It is taken from philosophy. I believe the existentialist style has been dominant in Europe since the 1920's and earlier, and certainly in this country since the Second World War and earlier also. But despite its earlier appearance, the style characterizes the twentieth century more than any other. I believe that as we speak about the eighteenth century and then mean immediately the style of enlightenment or rationalism and about the nineteenth century and think immediately of naturalism and scientism, the twentieth century will be seen later on in the light of this existentialist style. Now that is the general presupposition. It includes a very positively held valuation of this style in all realms of expression.

Now you ask me, does this style express the human situation better than any other? I do not know, but perhaps. Early Romanesque style[12] also did it very well and some late Gothic.[13] Bosch[14] and Bruegel[15] did it very well. But in any case this style is ours and we must understand it in order to understand ourselves. I believe that here, in a way which has no direct analogy in the past of the Western world, [humanity] expresses [its] predicament in a grandiose way without reconciling symbols. No reconciling symbols can be found or only a very few. There are some religious pictures which do not count very much. The whole development of the style is a self-interpretation of [humanity] from the point of view of [its] predicament: namely, what the existentialist themselves called estrangement of [humanity itself] from [its] true being, from the ground of [its] being, from others and from [itself], especially. In that respect, I believe, this century is a treasure chest of insights into the human situation, into the human predicament, as probably has not been found before, except maybe in some of the monastic literature in which a very refined search of the human reactions can be found, but that literature was forgotten.

Non-Objective Art

Now the last point you made refers to the so-called non-objective art. Such art belongs to the very interesting phenomenon that slowly [replaced the existentialist style]. Very early in the twentieth century Cubism starts to put the human figure into sections or mathematical or geometrical forms. Then the figure is disturbed more and more so that if you try to find out what it is, it is a riddle picture and you must guess its meaning. But this is not the way to look at it.

The way to look at non-objective art is to look at the underground elements out of which our reality is composed. It is a breaking through the surface of our ordinary experience with people and things in time and space. You have the same thing in poetry; you have it in drama; and you have it everywhere. This breakthrough is in itself an analogy to what I said about [humanity's] predicament.

Now the fact that [humanity] has disappeared as a figure is in itself a phenomenon. For instance, portraits have become more or less impossible on this basis. The human figure did not go so quickly. First, landscapes were still recognized, but then they also were dissolved. Then the organic beings -- animals and human bodies -- were put in pieces. Then the pieces were put in different places in the whole of the picture. For instance, one of the greatest German artists, Marc, has done this in a marvelous way.[16] Then the faces, more or less, were dissolved into the underground of nature. Then the whole figure disappeared, I mean, the bodily as well as the expression of the face. What was left were elements which are partly similar to what we find in microphysics -- the inquiry into the composition of atoms, molecules, and so on. Finally, even this was reduced to colors and lines and nothing of the figure was left.

Now what does this mean? It means a very radical restatement. The surface world has been dissolved, but we are now able to have the use of those elements out of which the surface world -- our daily world -- is composed. This underground replaces the other side. If you have great pictures of this kind, then you will see that these elements of reality have a metaphysical power. They have a real power which is so much greater than any of the so-called beautifying, naturalistic, religious pictures of the nineteenth century, which is the lowest status to which religious art had ever sunk. The reaction against this is a part of the present situation.

A year ago there was an exhibition in the Museum of Modern Art in New York under the title *New Images of Man* [sic]. I was asked to write the introduction to the catalog, and I did.[17] It was an exhibition of people, who with the stylistic means of present day nonobjective art, tried to elaborate again human forms and faces out of this material of stylistic forms. How far they succeeded I do not dare to say. I was not enthusiastic about the actual performance, but I was very positive about the attempt to follow the old word of God in the creation story, "Let us make [humanity] in an image like ours." These artists tried to help the elements of the human face to reemerge again out of the materials into which they had dissolved reality.

Here we are in the very beginning. We do not know what will come. The only thing I would hate, if it came, would be a simple restorative relapse to the horrors of the nineteenth century beautifuls (laughter). For the twentieth century and beyond, this would be unthinkable.

Picasso's *Guernica*

Question: Dr. Tillich, in your book on *Theology of Culture* you mentioned that the Protestant principle is best expressed b Picasso's painting *Guernica*. I wonder if you could enlarge on that please?

Dr. Tillich: I have already answered this question in print,[18] and now I do it again and again orally. My friend, Reinhold Niebuhr, who quoted this, forgot that in the statement in which I said that I said that 50% of *Guernica* is the most Protestant picture. The other 50% is not Protestant but is simply existentialist without an answer. Protestantism also gives an answer.

What I meant with the 50% was that we have here -- in the same way in which I describe it in this moment -- a breaking through the surface of a beautified reality and a showing of the horrors of what now is expressed in everybody's question: what about another world war and [humanity's] self-destruction of [humankind] to a large extent? The picture shows the horrors of war -- even the demonic presence of the bull and the other horrors of burning human bodies and a destroyed existence.

Now this, I would say, is a genuine Protestant way of seeing the human situation -- first of all without human consolation. There is no consolation by a church nor by a state nor by a pacifism nor by Utopia nor by a sentimental Jesus. The picture sees the human situation in the reality in which it is. I think that is what this picture performs and really has performed. It was awakened innumerable people in a way in which few others have done, but it remains a question and it does not give an answer.

Protestantism gives an answer. These words are the other 50% which usually are not quoted because this would make the statement less sensational (general laughter).

PROTESTANTISM'S LACK OF CATHOLIC SUBSTANCE

Question: Dr. Tillich, as an historian and a traditionalist, I am disturbed by the historical force of Protestantism. It seems to me that instead of attending to the roots which I see in the Catholic church, it has been busy cutting away its roots. So, I find Protestantism more rootless now than it was even a hundred years ago.

Then as an Anglo-Catholic, as I fancy myself to be, I see in the Catholic doctrine an assumption and concern and regard for the whole community which, to me, the individualism of Protestantism does not show. Yet I find myself here kind of sitting on a sword because I cannot accept the fulsomeness and the totality of the doctrine of Rome and yet I cannot accept the atomism that I think is implicit in Protestant doctrine.

Is there a chance for a return to a sacramental-confessional church with a regard and with a concern for the totality of the community -- not only a small community, but the human community, as well -- speaking for that and yet without the dogmatism and the authoritarianism that Rome represents?

Dr. Tillich: This was well spoken for the middle way -- the via media -- of the Episcopalian church. I understand your point of view very well and have expressed it in my own language as Protestant principle and Catholic substance, which must again come together. So I agree very intensively with your question. Not only as an historian, but also as a theologian, I would certainly agree with you. There is a way in which Protestantism has lost much of the substance, if I may use that word again here in a little bit different way, of the Catholic church, of the Catholic liturgy and symbolism and all these things.

RELIGION OF MORAL COMMANDS

Now we must distinguish here the development of Protestantism. That is one thing which I want to answer first. You refer to present day Protestantism which has become even more deprived of such substance than it was before. Here we agree. I believe that at least, perhaps, before the second World War, American Protestantism was a continuous repetition of moral commands. It was a religion of the so-called teachings of Jesus, which were identified with another Mosaic law which was only a little bit more refined. The meaning of the term Gospel -- namely, evangelon, which means good news -- was completely forgotten.

From their early years onward, Protestant children were put under the law. The message of forgiveness, of grace, of a new reality which has come through Christianity was not preached to them, at least not with such a strength that they were able to understand the difference between the Old and New Testament. In this way Protestantism became largely a moral education institute and the Sunday schools were the way in which this was supposed to be done. I think this happened more in this country than in most other Protestant countries. One did not learn what Christianity is.

One did not learn that Christianity is first of all the acceptance of those who are unacceptable. That is the whole teaching of the New Testament, and nothing of this remained. It was the good pious people, "people of good will" as the terrible phrase says, who are supposedly those who are near to God and the others are supposedly under [God's] condemnation. Now this is the one hundred-eighty degrees turning around of the message of the New Testament. I agree with you that this was one of the worst things which Protestantism largely has experienced.

A REDISCOVERY OF THE SYMBOLIC TRADITION

I do not think it is so bad any longer because such awareness of this situation is in the whole younger generation of theologians. One of the symptoms of this is that they really try to understand the Reformation, which was the reestablishment of the good news of forgiveness and acceptance. They are interested in expressing this not in commands and not in doctrines but in symbols. There is a great interest today in all Protestant groups for a rediscovery of the symbolic tradition of the church.

Now all this is in line with what the Anglican church has always tried to do -- namely, to find a middle way between the Roman church without the authority of the Pope and Protestantism without the rationalistic, ethical and intellectual element in the later Martin Luther himself but also in later Protestantism. So I agree with you, but now where do we find this unity?

The Protestant principle excludes the possibility of the Pope because it puts every church under the divine judgment. It makes it impossible for it to be an infallible institution. It makes it impossible for anything, including doctrine and liturgy, to be immovable. These all are in history. They all are under judgment, and none of them should claim to be absolute. The Catholic substance is the expression of this [unity] in the great tradition of cultic and doctrinal ideas. I worked for this from the point of view of theology, many others from the point of view of the cult and the rituals, others from the point of view of ethics, and so on. We try to bring in as many elements of the Catholic tradition as possible. But there is something difficult in it. I will come to your question in two ways, especially since you said you are Anglo-Catholic.

DIFFICULTY WITH CATHOLIC SUBSTANCE

I have more friends and pupils in the Episcopalian church, I believe, than in any other, including my own -- the Lutheran, originally, and now the Evangelical and Reformed. They often ask me, "Why don't you become an Episcopalian because, with this slogan of Protestant principle and Catholic substance, you have so much in common with?" The reason I do not is that you can go a via media -- a middle way -- only if you have experienced the extreme ways. That is my criticism of the Anglican church.

I can prove that in theology. For instance, Anglicanism never dared to go to the radical questions. Therefore, it is very backward in theology. The Germans are wild people, I know that (laughter), even in theology, but they dare to go to the extremes. They dare to think radically. The British are much better behaved people (laughter). They go to extremes much less, but they do not have these experiences which finally make for the fact, which nobody can deny, that most of the theology since the beginning of the nineteenth century came from Germany. It came neither from this country nor from Great Britain. It is probably so in all the different things.

The via media is possible only if the reala extrema have been used. This has not happened. Therefore, I see that the Anglican church tells us something. It keeps the situation of the tremendous loss in Protestantism before us, but it does not really give to the majority of Protestants an answer which says, "Now we come to you." That is impossible.

So I would say, I see your problem very much. I would like a new via media by which we could go, but you are only the via media which never went to the extremes, and that we cannot follow.

FOOTNOTES

1.   "Culture and Religion" originally appeared in *Foundations: A Baptist Journal of History and Theology,* Vol. XIV, No. 1, January-March, 1971, pp. 6-17, with inclusive language added.

2.   In a memorial tribute to Professor Tillich, James Luther Adams spoke of "the light and warmth of responsive fellowship" that so many experienced with him. For Tillich, the give-and-take of dialogue was "a manifestation of the power of being." As a

result of his experience as a student of talking late into the night when he was Privatodozent in Berlin, Tillich introduced what he called "discussion breaks," even during his lectures, "a practice that was not customary at the time." (James Luther Adams, "Words for Paul Tillich," *Harvard Divinity Bulletin,* January, 1966, 30, 20, p. 9)

3. By "spiritual" (capital "S") Tillich means the divine Spirit; by "spiritual" (lower case "s"), he means the human spirit.

4. "The Experiential, The Theological and Psychotherapy," in this volume.

5. In *A History of Christian Thought* (Edited by Carl E. Braaten. London: SCM Press, 1968), Tillich observed that "we have the most translucent religious art in the Byzantine mosaics. These mosaics have no tendency at all to describe everything which happens in the horizontal line. They want to express the presence of the divine through everything which appears on the horizontal level of reality, on the place of time and space, by making everything a symbol pointing to its own depth." In Byzantine art the predominant theme was the majesty of Christ. Its conception of reality emphasized "the significance of an event rather than its appearance." (Helen Gardner's *Art Through the Ages.* Fourth edition. Revised under Sumner McK. Crosby. New York: Harcourt, Brace and Company, 1959, p. 207)

6. Could Tillich have been referring to the Church of San Marco in Florence, rather than the Cathedral of San Marco in Venice? It is especially noted for its Renaissance high altarpiece of the Virgin and Child enthroned with saints and angels painted by Fra Angelico in 1438 A.D. (Gardner, op. cit., pp. 303, 304)

7. Japanese Buddhist art tends to portray quiet repose, suffering, and sorrow, whereas Christian art tends to portray sin, tragedy and salvation.

8. Tillich interpreted the fully developed mystical system of the Neo-Platonists as "the ecstasy of the individual person leads to a

union with the One, with the Absolute, with God." The idea expressed the break-up of all particular religions and simultaneously "the impossibility for reason to create by itself a new content of life." Augustine found a new certainty in the Neo-Platonic philosophy that "you have the immediacy of truth in the inner soul."

9.   The doctrine of Creation distinguished Christianity from paganism. "Creation out of nothing means that God did not find an already pre-existent matter when [God] started to create. There was no matter which resists form, as it was in Neo-Platonic paganism, and which must therefore be transcended. Instead, the material world is an object of God's creation; it is good and must not be disparaged for the sake of salvation." (See Tillich, op. cit., p. 20)

10.   In discussing the existentialist aspects of modern art, Tillich observed that "most modern art as transformed all of reality into forms of still life ... organic forms have disappeared, and with them has disappeared idealism which always is connected with the description of the organic forms. The forms of our existence are no more organic. They are atomistic, disrupted. These disrupted forms of our existence are taken by themselves by modern artists as the real elements of reality ... Cubic forms are the unorganic forms out of which the world is constituted. But the artists do not accept the statement that these forms are only unorganic. Embodied in this very unorganic form is the power of being itself. In this way the disruptedness of expressionism, surrealism, and all the other recent forms of style, such as cubism and futurism, is nothing else than an attempt to look into the depths of reality, below any surface and any beautification of the surface and any organic unity. It is the attempt to see the elements of reality as fundamental powers of being out of which reality is constructed." (Carl Michaelson, Ed. *Christianity and The Existentialists.* New York: Charles Scribner's Sons, 1956, pp. 136-137) For a complete analysis of his views, see Paul Tillich, *On Art and Architecture.*

Edited and with an Introduction by John Dillenberger, in collaboration with Jane Dillenberger (New York: Crossroads, 1987).

11. Paul Cezanne (1839-1906) was the forerunner of Cubism by his use of "transparent forms to expose basic inner structures." Even though he had earlier utilized the Impressionists' search for luminosity, it remained form and distance that held his attention in his exploration of permanent values. "Always in search of basic truths, he concentrated less on naturalistic appearances than on the nature of underlying form." (See Katherine Kuh, *Break-Up: The Core of Modern Art.* Greenwich, Connecticut: New York Graphic Society, 1965, p. 39)

12. In Romanesque style the artist distorts the human figure in order to convey an emotion or idea. Thus the style may be called expressionistic. The Romanesque period of the 11th and 12th centuries was a time of great upheaval because of the invasions of Northern barbarian tribes and the weakening of the political, social, and economic structure. Varying degrees of classical, barbarian, and Byzantine elements are welded together in the emerging style. The massive stone walls of the churches and fortresses "express the need for security." In both monasticism and feudalism, which reached their peaks at this time, there was the attempt "to establish self-sufficient communities and to withdraw from or ward off contact with the world at large." The portrayed anguish of the damned or those destroyed by scourges and pestilences have "the urgency and anguish of the twentieth century *Guernica* by Picasso." (Gardner, op. cit., pp. 228-242)

13. The late Gothic period is generally linked with the disruptions and dismay of the late 14th and 15th centuries. Pessimism, delusion, and frantic gaiety appeared to possess the people. "The faith of the thirteenth century gave way to pietism, to an accent on mysticism and to dramatic representations, both in liturgical drama and mystery plays, of the sufferings of Christ or of martyrs and saints." (See Gardner, op. cit., p. 279.)

14. Hieronymous Bosch (ca. 1450-1516) was a unique painter in the Flemish tradition. "In his dream world, prefiguring the nightmare landscapes of modern Surrealists, real and unreal are equally believable," says Gardner (op. cit., pp. 383-384) Bosch displayed a passion and genius for the distorted, the grotesque, the macabre, the exuberant. The demon called desire runs riot. What one sees is a kind of cosmic shipwreck in which "everything breaks up, falls asunder, scatters" and then is reassembled. All parts and voices are equally divided, equally insistent in their separate claims yet all are maintained "in perfect equilibrium." The latent ambivalences and basic ambiguity in [humanity's] imagination come across as a delight and a puzzle. (See Robert L. Delevoy, *Bosch.* Cleveland: World Publishing Company, n.d., pp. 65, 78, 41, 94)

15. Pieter Bruegel the Elder (1525/30-1569) also had his roots in the native Flemish tradition. His pictures exhibit a strong sense of peasant robustness, seeming to preclude the intellectualizing and affected elegance practiced by his contemporaries in the North. (Gardner, op. cit., pp. 384-385) His subject matter ranged "from good cheer to near tragedy, from grotesque Flemish fantasies and comic illustrated proverbs to landscapes so universal that they seem to be philosophical statements about the dependence of [humanity] upon nature." His intensity of meaning and vividness of invention approach Bosch in his nightmarish monsters. His paragons of virtue at times "carry virtue to the point of foolish excess ... behaving with a zeal so fanatical that it amounts to sinfulness." (Timothy Foote, *The World of Bruegel c. 1959-1569.* New York: Time-Life Books, 1968, pp. 15, 80)

Tillich (Michaelson, op. cit., pp. 140-141) wrote of "those great demonic pictures by Bruegel and Bosch where elements of the psychological as well as the natural reality are brought into the picture without a naturalistic connection with each other, without a system of categories into which they are put. This is the all-important element in existentialism. The essential categories, time, space, causality, substance have lost their ultimate power."

16.   Franz Marc (1880-1916) was "perhaps the most sensitive of the German Expressionists." (Gardner, op. cit., p. 700) He separated local color from the original object. His transcendental interests can be seen in his attempt to penetrate "the organic structure of things." "I am trying to intensity my feelings for the organic rhythm of all things," he wrote, "to achieve pantheistic empathy with the throbbing and flowering of nature's blood stream -- in trees, in animals, in the air." For him, rhythm meant "the structural laws of the individual being, the vital order of the species, the harmony of all created things." He shattered "life's mirror," as he put it, "to look directly into being." (Klaus Lankheit, *Franz Marc: Watercolors, Drawings, Writings.* New York: Harry N. Abrams, Inc. 1960, pp. 14, 15, 1)

17.   See "A Prefatory Note to New Images of Man [sic]." In Tillich, op. cit., 1987, pp. 241-243.

18.   See Michaelson, op. cit., pp. 137-138; Tillich op. cit., 1987, pp. 95-96, 179.

CULTURE AND THEOLOGY[1]

BEYOND LIBERALISM AND CONSERVATISM

Question: Dr. Tillich, while you were talking, you reminded me of an article which you wrote two or three years ago called "Beyond the Usual Alternatives."[2] I think it is in that article that you are implying that the liberals had gone to one extreme and that the neo-orthodox had reacted from them, but that neither position seemed to satisfy you and that there were new questions and new trends. Would you develop a little farther what you think the new trends and new points of emphasis are that should be made in the near future?

Dr. Tillich: Now you also ask me for a <u>via media</u> (laughter).[3] But this time it is not in the universal sense between Protestantism and Catholicism, but in the more narrow sense within Protestant theology between the conservative and the liberal lines of thought. I do not remember this article clearly (general laughter), but in any case I speak from the present moment.

I believe that the alternative which plagued our early studies in Germany in the first decade of this century is obsolete. I think that even Karl Barth would think so. It is simply historically not valid any more. Of course in saying this, I must dismiss quite a lot of ideas and must express my own ideas. If you allow me to do this, I will try to show it in a few points.

The Historical-Critical Approach

Now one of the points which has produced most of the discussions in this country -- and now again in Germany where it was already equally alive a hundred years ago -- is the question of an historical approach to the Biblical literature. This was usually understood as the domain of the liberal theology.

There was the fact of the discovery of the sources. There was the discovery and distinguishing of the three different elements in all biblical literature -- the historical element, the legendary element, the mythological element. There was the question of the historical development of the literature -- what is early, what is late, who are the authors and all these things. Now that was done by (what was called for a hundred years) liberal or critical theology. I would say this approach is now a common good. The method has been accepted whether somebody is a little bit more critical or a little bit more conservative in historical research. You have the same thing if you go to the sources of Greek or Roman history or of the medieval figure. You can be more trustful of the sources or more critical of the sources, but that is a matter of quantity and not of quality. The decisive thing is the historical approach. In serious theology it is generally accepted. This means that the rejection of the liberal side of your alternative at this point is not necessary any more. The discussion about this is in itself a theological foundation of all thinking.

Then the other side is the systematic theology. Here liberal theology tried to construe a system of theological doctrines, which were completely unsatisfactory. Very early they were discovered to be unsatisfactory. Their unsatisfactoriness was already anticipated in Germany in the years when I was a student and then [experienced] definitely in the 1920's when the two main representatives of liberal theology -- namely, Harnack and Troeltsch -- died and Karl Barth took over. In this moment, the inadequacy of systematics in the liberal theology became very obvious. From that time on the new development was going on in all theology.

Orthodox Theology

Now consider the other side, the reaction. I do not speak of fundamentalists. In Europe, they are called immovable Orthodoxy. I do not consider them to be serious partners in theological discussion today. The problem was much more refined. As in all sciences, some older questions and problems become obsolete because of new ideas and discoveries. So it was also the case in theology.

Now the theology of Karl Barth -- the so-called and badly named dialectical theology -- came up. In this country it is called neo-orthodoxy. That designation is partly true because it was a reaffirmation of many elements in classical orthodoxy, which was a great theology.[4] Classical theology is as great as that of the medieval scholastics, and it was completely forgotten by many of the younger generation.

I would like every student to read at least one of the classical orthodox people from the seventeenth and late sixteenth centuries. Then he [or she] would have a basis for theological thought, even if [one] is radically critical. At least then [one] would have the material against which [one] could be critical. But now even our criticism is in the air. It does not have the real theological material against which it is directed. So this was my praise of orthodoxy. This was serious theology.

Barth himself is not an orthodox. He is called neo-orthodox. This is a misnomer; dialectical is a misnomer; perhaps, theology of crisis is a better name. In any case it is Barthian theology. Everybody knows that here some elements are reemphasized in ways which united him with what we discussed before as existentialist theology, philosophy, and art. That is, the human predicament is taken radically seriously. The optimistic elements in liberal systematic theology -- which ultimately came from the eighteenth century, especially, from some elements in Kant, although not from all of them -- were completely negated and denied by the Barthian theology. So he was not old orthodox. In some way he was existentialist and in some way, of course, traditional.

So, I would say, we must now remove those [optimistic] elements from this movement. I myself confess that I was deeply influenced by Karl Barth's first prophetic book, *The Commentary on St. Paul's Epistle to the Romans,* which was, of course, the development of his own attack on his church and theology on the basis of the text of Paul. It was a book which was a shaking of the foundation of the whole liberal systematic thinking at that time. It was a great thing, but it was not orthodox in the ordinary sense of the word.

I believe [the following] is the way we have to go. We have to accept the results of critical history with respect to the Biblical books. We have to build a theology which is able to give an answer to the questions as developed by our existentialist thinking, acting, painting, philosophy, and everything. If this is done, then, I believe, that the old alternative [between liberalism and conservatism] really has become obsolete, which it deserves to be.

Radicalize the Questions

Question: I would like to ask you to go back to the proposition that there can be a via media only if you have gone to the extremes. I would like to know why this is so. I can imagine the reaction of an Anglican could be, "This is arbitrary; this is a simulated rule of yours, but is it really manifestly true? You might only appeal to people who had gone to the extremes if you had also gone to the extremes. Since the majority of people have not gone to the extremes, maybe the via media is a way of saving them from having to go to the extremes."

Dr. Tillich: Now the word "extremes" sounds very extreme (general laughter). I do not mean it as badly as it sounds. Let me go back to the example of theology. A theology which never took seriously the historical question, which I just discussed, cannot give an answer to the problems which are implied in this question.

By the way, this is my real criticism of Karl Barth. He also did not take the historical problem so seriously. Thus, he was surprised when his pupil and friend Bultmann again brought up the whole question and called it demythologization of the Bible, of the New Testament: namely, the removal of the mythological elements.

If, out of necessity, you have never radically applied historical rules -- or, in this case, I would even say honestly applied historical rules -- of methodical research, then you cannot know what is involved. You then say, "I keep away from such radical criticism. I think some words of Jesus are very guaranteed; they are very probably true or certainly true; there may be a few which are not."

This kind of sedative drugs in thinking is not good for human beings if they really think this way. That prevents them from experiencing the depths of life. If you use these sedatives in historical research, you will never see the deep problems the state of the Gospel records gives us with respect to Christian theology and the tremendous weight these problems have if you deal with their consequences. You will not be able to build up a theology of any power because you do not have a radical question to answer. You answer only very preliminary questions that do not go very far and so you have nice answers.

This is not the way history goes and, especially, thought. If all our great physicists, for instance, had not asked very radical questions -- as [did] Newton, Galileo, Einstein and now the quantum theoreticians -- we would not have gone beyond the earlier states and would be in a limited realm. Einstein radicalized the question of relativity, for instance, in such a way that a new view of reality came out, which certainly is not the end but is a point which had to be reached in order to go on. In the same way, I have meant it with the realm of thinking.

Probably the same [radicalized question] is necessary with respect to the liturgical problem. It will be nice news in your ears (laughter) to know that I myself belonged to a liturgical movement in Germany. We called it Berneuchen,[5] according to a little Eastern German village where we met. We were a group of people in the twenties who worked for liturgical enrichment and reform. We threw out the distorted liturgies of the nineteenth century, sentimental hymns of the same kind, and, of course, the very minor paintings and so on, and tried to bring a renewal in this respect.

Then the puzzling and very difficult question arose: namely, how far can you go back and take old liturgical traditions and reintroduce them, even if they are purified against the theological and aesthetic distortions that always happen in history?

In this Berneuchen movement there were two wings. The one was almost unrestricted with respect to using the treasures of the old church and trying to introduce them into the present Protestant Germany. This actually meant Lutheran liturgies. There was the other group, to which I and some other friends belonged, who said, "The liturgies must be understandable by the German workers, for instance. Are these phrases -- produced by the Greek church fathers, who had highly aesthetic feeling and great power -- understandable? Is there anything which you can tell them in their daily loves, their political struggle, their misery, their form of life which is shaped on the lowest and ugliest level? What can you do with these?"

So our struggle went on and on. I cannot judge the present situation. There is an extreme wing in this movement which is still very much alive and radically liturgical. It goes back to everything it can get of the past. There are those who resist it. Here you see one of the profound problems of this easy slogan "Protestant principle and religious [Catholic] substance."

THE QUEST FOR COMMUNITY

Question: In conjunction with the question raised before concerning our quest for community in Protestant faith today, I have recently noticed increasing emphasis among our Christian groups for the quest for Christian community as such. However, we are often reminded by our secular colleagues in the behavioral sciences that since the Renaissance our negative approach of freedom left the atomization of individuals with increasing insecurity -- hence, our escape from freedom. If this Christian faith is [humanity's] confrontation with God alone and naked in a dyadic situation, how would you view this current Protestant request for community? Is it a positive search for this real human and Christian fellowship or it is one of the manifestations again in our society to cover our essential insecurity to face God alone and naked?

Dr. Tillich: There are different movements, as far as I know, here and also certainly in Germany, which call themselves Koinonia, which is the Greek word for community.

There are many communities or Koinonias in which we all stand. There is the family community. There is the neighborhood community. There are communities of student groups. I myself belong to one of them in Germany, a Christian corporation or a Christian Fraternity as you would call it, which was of highest importance.[6] There are others like this.

And there is the church, which is supposed to be a community and largely is not what it is supposed to be. In every apostolic creed it confesses that. The Koinonia is the community of the saints -- not meaning that they are good people of good will or something like that. It means they belong to the group which exists by the very fact that it is on the basis of the New Being and of belonging to the New Being. But this is the reality. That is not escape in itself.

You would not say that the Koinonia of family is an escape. It is first of all a reality, but it can become an escape. Often people who suffer under the meaninglessness of their business life or of their life as clerks in a regulated form of existence return to the lap of their families. There they try to find the anti-atomization situation.

Escape or Genuine?

Now when is this genuine and when is this escape? It is very hard to define that. You cannot do it in general terms.

You can say that sometimes it is a continuation of the atomization when the social structure reaches into the family itself and separates children from parents and man from wife, making each of them a business subject or an autonomous subject. They meet sometimes, but the community, the Koinonia, is gone. So this is a possibility. Then it is not even an escape. It is less than an escape. It is not a solution in any respect. That is possible.

On the other hand, it can be a genuine community where the term escape would be completely inadequate. I mean: I have the experience of love; I have friendships; I have family. I would say these experiences of love and friendship are not escapes from anything. At least I am not aware of this in any way. My relationship to my students and many other things are not escapes at all.

These relationships become escapes only if they are used as means to overcome the catastrophic situation in the society as a whole, namely, what you call the atomization. Then these relationships are not human in their genuine quality, as something which in itself is positive, but are there only in order to flee from something else, which is daily life. For instance, the inner intensities are eaten up so much by our business life in the largest sense of the word -- including all professions, including professor of theology -- that intensity, the concentration, going into the family life is lacking. Then, of course, it becomes an escape and nothing else.

The same is true with the church. In itself it is a Koinonia of those who have a common faith in something, something which naturally happens in every society, all the time. Groups of common conviction come together and strengthen each other. All this is natural and right. The church should be the most universal and the most fundamental of these communities because it is a matter of ultimate concern. All the others, even family, is a preliminary concern in relationship to the ultimate.

So the question is not whether they are escapes. The question is: under which conditions can they, must they, be considered to be escapes?

Suburban Piety

Here I could refer, for instance, to the famous problem of suburban piety. Suburban piety means including the church in the socially security systems -- the psychological social security systems. You are social secure because you go to church every Sunday and have your nice talk afterwards. Then you belong to those who do that, and the others are people of bad will.

Now this kind of fact, I would call escape. But even here I try to be fair. I would say there are many weak people. I think in our Western culture, especially here in America, there are very many very weak people, as the psychotherapeutic situation shows. For them, it often may be a real help to be supported -- psychologically, I mean now -- by a group to which they belong. Because they do not have the power of being autonomous or non-conformists, shall we let them go down or shall we say, "Now here they can find a group in which the weaker are carried by the stronger?"

I ask this, although I would say this kind of suburban Christianity is one of the greatest dangers for Protestantism just because it is positive and not negative. But it is positive on a basis which is not the real problem of ultimate concern. Half of it is the means for social standing and things like that. Even so, I would say, do not underestimate the support which, in such a Koinoinia as the church, the strong ones give to the weak ones. Here the word escapism is said a little bit from the kind of arrogant superiority feeling which is not always justified.

DEMYTHOLOGY AND VITAL SYMBOLS

Question: You mentioned in the problem of liturgy for your group whether it would be according to the past or trying to make things relevant. This brings up, through the back door, the problem of demythology. Are you in agreement with Bultmann, which I gather you might be by what you said about making things relevant? On the other hand, if you are not, how are the Christian images and communications, words and myths, to be revitalized, because they are not merely conscious descriptions? If they are alive, they express the depths of the human spirit.

Dr. Tillich: Now I am in agreement, as you inferred from what I said, with Bultmann with respect to his historical method -- simply showing what is probably history. It is all probability. We can never go beyond probability: probably this is history; probably this is legend; probably this is myth. Now you can say this and it has been said so often that I think we must accept it, although about every special point there may be different interpretations. If this is called demythologization, I would say I am in full agreement with Bultmann and have often told him this.

Then the second element is the question: does this mean that the religious language should be deprived of its mythological elements -- that means, of its symbols? I would say, by no means. Then we would have no religious language. Religious language is the language of the symbol and the myth. I define myth as a set of symbols combined into a story. Of course, without this, no religious statement could be made at all. Even the term God is not a religious statement. It is probably a nonsensical philosophical statement. In any case we must use these symbols.

Today these symbols still have (for many people who accept them and many who reject them) the connotation of literal meaning, of literalism. They are taken as events in time and space, which a good *Time* reporter, who also had some psycho-photographic apparatus to see the inner movement, would probably be able to see and would report as well as most *Time* reporters report their stories. Now if you bring the Gospel down to such a level of inter-empirical relationships, then, of course, you must be absolutely credulous and superstitious in order to accept them. If you are not this, you must reject them as radically on the other hand.

But this is not the situation, and I think that is the meaning of your question. The situation is that we cannot miss the great symbols and are not able to replace them intentionally. No symbol can be produced intentionally. It comes out of something which one might call the collective unconscious and is not a matter of our good will or bad will. If this is the case, we must use them. If we use them, we must not demythologize them but deliteralize them. That is what I told Bultmann. He should not have used that word. Instead he should have used the word deliteralize: namely, taking away the literal understanding of symbols and myths.

Religions Education and Deliteralization

How can this be done? You have actually asked a much larger question perhaps than you were aware in this moment: namely, the question of religions education generally. In religious education the problem is what do we give our children? Here the whole thing becomes concrete.

It became concrete for myself more than in my New Testament study. It became concrete in the moment in which you are before the question: shall you give the children in their early years the symbols which you know in our world will become objects of doubt very soon? Some people think (and I had the same feeling) you had better keep them away and give them later when they can understand their nonliteral meaning. I would say it was a mistake.

I think that the symbols must enter the subconscious of the children as early as possible and as strongly as possible. Then, of course, the critical questioning period comes. In view of this, tomorrow I would probably have to dismiss fifty percent of the Sunday School teachers. They often -- I heard again and again to my horror; I could not believe it, and finally I had to believe it -- forbid their children to ask questions about the truth and the validity of these stories and these symbols. Now if they do this, I would say they should not stay in this service one day longer. But if they do the other thing, then they can be the most important helpers for the Christian Churches: namely, to deliteralize the symbols which are given to the children in the early years.

Somehow you can do this even if you stay in the Biblical literature. The Fourth Gospel is a continuous demythologization or deliteralization of many ideas which we find in the first three Gospels. They already had the same problem at that time. They started demythologizing, for instance, the eschatology, the doctrine of the end of history and all these beautiful images of the seven seals,[7] and all this. Now the Fourth Gospel tells, [whoever] accepts me here and how in this moment already has the eternal life; and [whoever] does not falls under the judgment which is going on now.[8] This is demythologization or better deliteralization of the fantastic forms of the traditional eschatology. Such things already go on in the Bible and then in the classical theology again and again with respect to the idea of God and Christ and so on.

Now why cannot we do this today? I would say we can, but we must first be awakened to the problem. We can do it only if we believe that these symbols are still the most powerful expressions of our way of expressing our ultimate concern. If we believe that and then know about the situation and want to communicate with our children, then I think we can do a great work. We poor theologians only have the job of making the job of the Sunday School teacher a little bit easier.

The Lord's Supper and Deliteralization

Question: Mr. Tillich, how would you apply this deliteralization to a view of the Eucharist that would embrace the real presence? By this, I mean, it seems to me that Protestants are faced with either the idea of a memorial service pure and simple or of an Eucharistic service in which the real presence is there. Do you think it is possible to apply a kind of deliteralization to the doctrine of the real presence so that you do not have to accept literally the concept of the body and blood and yet which, in a sense, symbolically but not commemoratively has been accepted?

Dr. Tillich: Now this is a good example of the problem so that I would like to go into it. First of all, the memorial idea is the idea of Zwingli, which has never had great influence on the whole of Protestantism. There was the alternative between Zwingli and Calvin in continental thought. Anglicanism was even more on the side of the Catholic form than Luther himself. That is the first thing. So we do not need to worry very much about what you call commemorative.

Question: Does not the Baptist church follow this?

Dr. Tillich: Yes, of course. They, I believe, are even very critical of the sacramental idea altogether. Early Baptists in the Reformation period are called sacramentarians because they denied all sacraments (general laughter).

In any case, the real problem seems to me to be the following. In the discussion between Zwingli and Luther -- where the question was discussed in one of the most important conferences -- in Marburg, 1529, the words were difficult. Zwingli said, "Bread and wine are symbols." Against this Luther said, "No, they are the blood and body of Christ."

Now philologically, the interpretation of "this is my blood" is, of course, according to the Hebrew kind of thinking, as people have explained long ago. It means "significant." It means "signifies." But this literal interpretation is not the problem. The problem here is the term "real."

Now if you take "really real," then you come to such absurdities that you yourself would like to demythologize in the next moment because what does "real" mean here? "Real" is my body. This is not the body of Christ. If you say it is the transcendent body, what does that mean? Luther drove to the consequence; it is ubiquitous. The body of Christ is everywhere: here in this table; now in this moment, but only shows itself in the sacrament. At that time even this was condemned as absurd, although it had some depth in it. Now let's leave out this kind of literalistic, I would call it, absurdity and understand what really is meant.

What is really meant is that the Christ Spirit, as Paul calls it -- Christ the Spirit -- is present in the actual symbols which are given in the sacrament. It is not a memory of something which happened once upon a time and which we cannot remember anyhow because we were not present. It is not even a memory in thinking of a recorded story. But it is the idea that as God -- that always means His spirit -- is present to us in a sermon or in a reading of the Bible when it is the divine Spirit which hits us, so [God] is present in these visible things, which are not words but visible realities. This is what real presence means over against the commemorative thing. To this I would hold, not only with respect to the Lord's Supper but also the water of Baptism and to many other things which are symbols.

In other words, "symbol" in the discussion in Marburg was meant or understood as what we today would understand as sign, a "mere" sign. You can say a "mere" sign. You never can say a "mere" symbol because nothing is more realistic than a symbol. Therefore, if bread and wine are symbols that are accepted by the collective unconscious of the Christian Church under the effect of the divine presence, which we call the Holy Spirit, then, of course, we can say there is the real presence of the divine Spirit. But if we go beyond this, then these become absurdities.

Now you ask, what about the body and the blood? The body and the blood simply mean -- as in the Incarnation word of the Fourth Gospel -- "The Word became flesh." That means, not a sense of my flesh substance, of my muscular substance, but it means historical reality. In this sense, I would say the historical picture of Jesus as the Christ is present with his full individual reality which shines through with force. This reality is the bearer of the Spirit -- that, I would say, means the body here and everywhere.

If we now make a kind of higher physics out of the body of Christ -- transcendent osteology as it has been called (osteology meaning doctor of bones), this is something which must be rejected radically. And so I think we can.

If we use the word "real presence," then we must define what "real" means here. Otherwise it becomes absurd.

THE NEW BEING AND SOCIETY-AT-LARGE

Question: Dr. Tillich, you said that we needed to find an answer to the problem of this fragmented society. Through your concept of the New Being, are you suggesting this as an answer -- that each individual can become a new being through [one's] total involvement in society?

Dr. Tillich: First, let me say a few words about the term New Being. I do not say New Being, but I say a New Being as a power which can renew individuals and can renew groups including the Christian Church, which needs as much renewal each time as every individual needs renewal. Therefore, the word New Being means a state of reality in which the power of what has appeared in Jesus as the Christ has become the principle of that community in its living and acting and thinking. That is New Being. The individual enters the New Being and can then also become a new being [oneself] namely, a new individual [oneself] through this.

Now how is all this related to the larger community, namely, to all society at large? This is what I understand you want to know. This is related in two ways.

Basic Reality

The one side is this. In the Christian Church there is in the midst of our society a reality which points beyond the society, beyond any finite context, and which in its basic message and power is independent of anything that happens. Therefore, participation in the Church, which may be manifest or which may be latent (as I often say) -- this communion of those who are driven by the divine Spirit -- is a reality in our society which consents to society by participating in it yet which makes us independent of the destiny of the society. That is the decisive thing which the Christians experienced in the Roman Empire, which was in the process of demonic destruction (and perhaps today [humanity] is in the process of demonic destruction). In any case, the Church was certain that all this destructive process could not conquer the basic reality: namely, the image of the Christ or the message of the Christ through his image.

That, then, is the one side. This is the side which you, perhaps, would call escape. I would call it the basis for existence in a society which is open to a continuous fight between demonic and divine powers and in which one cannot say which will prevail in history itself. According to the Biblical message, in history the demonic will prevail. The end is identical with the great sufferings, the catastrophes, the rule of the demonic powers, the destruction which follows it and so on. Only in the transcendent is there the victory of the divine side. Now that is the Biblical view of history. Our time has more understanding of this view than one could have fifty years ago.

Ambiguous Reality

Now there is the other side. This side must be emphasized equally. From this reality -- to the degree in which it is alive -- there is a power going through all history which I would call saving power. It is not only alive in Western Christianity; it is also alive as the latent church everywhere where revelatory experiences have reunited God and [humanity]. This saving power has its immediate place in the latent or manifest church. From there, continuous influences go into society.

But these influences -- we spoke about it long before we spoke about Christian culture -- are all ambiguous and fragmentary. They are never so that you can say, "Here is the Kingdom of God." "Not here." "It is always around the corner." "The day after tomorrow it will come." That is the Utopian illusion which has produced so much disappointment and has tremendously strengthened the existentialist mood in our century. So this we cannot say. We can say that there is a continuous influence.

We must say there are these two sides. There is this influence; we must strengthen it. All of us try to do it. I mean, I try to do it in teaching a philosophy in the evaluation of arts, and all this. Others do it in more active forms as in politics. I even tried that -- not too successfully (general laughter). I gave you an example of what might be possible. So we influence everywhere, but we must always be aware of the fact that this is fragmentary; this is ambiguous. Therefore, the real certainty is not this but the presence of the eternal in the temporal.

Present Reality

The church as the witness to this eternal has something which, I would say with the words of Jesus, "the threshold of hell cannot conquer." It is in itself based on the presence of the ultimate, which cannot be conquered by anything finite. But any special Christian church can go down. Protestantism can come to an end. Roman Catholicism has come to an end as Catholicism, namely, as universal. All this is absolutely possible. But the message in itself is an expression of the presence of the divine and can only come to an end with the end of [humanity] itself, when the memory is extinguished and, perhaps, the few savages start all history again. I do not know whether that will happen. We must take everything into possible consideration.

I will conclude with a discussion I had with a friend -- a theologian, a great and tragic figure in theology. He said to me, "If the atomic bomb or something equal in collision with other stars would bring history to an end tomorrow, then I would say history has no sense. There is no meaning in history."

I said, "There is no date set when [humankind] or all life on earth will come to an end. But whether this is nearer or farther away from our present moment does not mean anything for the meaning of history itself, because this meaning is present in every moment. It is present in the moment in which I talk to you here and now."

This is my position. Therefore, from a theological point of view, I am not worried about the atomic destruction, even if it would be one hundred percent or if it would extinguish the memory of all history. I am not worried about whatever may come. If it happens in some time ahead that the earth becomes cold or some cosmic events occur or people become even more foolish than we are and destroy themselves, then I would still say, the Rock of Ages -- if you want a poetic expression of it which I like very much -- is beyond the ages because it is eternal.

If we have nothing in the vertical line which cannot be undercut by anything which happens in history, then I would say we have real cause for despair in the present world situation.

FOOTNOTES

1.   "Culture and Theology" originally appeared in *Foundations: A Baptist Journal of History and Theology,* Vol. XIV, No. 2, April-June, 1971, pp. 102-115, with inclusive language added.

2.   *The Christian Century,* May 7, 1958, pp. 553-555.

3.   Tillich and the good-humored response are in the context of the previous discussion in "Religion and Culture" of Anglo-Catholicism as an unacceptable via media because it failed to go to the extremes.

4.   "The immediate wave which followed the Reformation is the period of orthodoxy. Orthodoxy is greater and more serious than what is called fundamentalism in America. Fundamentalism is the product of a reaction in the nineteenth century, and is a primitivized form of classical Orthodoxy." Orthodoxy systematized and consolidated Reformation ideas. (Carl E. Braaten, edited, *A History of Christian Thought.* London: SCM Press, 1968, p. 275)

"The doctrinal element became much more important in Orthodoxy than in the Reformation, where the spiritual element was more decisive than the fixed doctrines." (Ibid., p. 278)

5. Berneuchen is the name of an estate in Neumark which was made available in 1923, by its owner, Rudolf von Viebohn, for a series of five conferences that continued until 1928. The movement began earlier, and arose in connection with the "Union of German Youth Association" (Bund Deutscher Jugendnereine), founded in 1909, and with the drastic failure of a large conference of youth leaders held early in 1923, in the Augern castle near Magdeburg, to deal with the problem posed by the fact that youth generally were not active in the Protestant Church. In the wake of the latter, Karl Bernhard Ritter and five other youth leaders arranged a smaller invitational conference at Berneuchen in May, 1923. The results of this and subsequent conferences held at Berneuchen were put down without identification of the participants in the *Berneuchner Buch* (1926). (*Die Religion in Geschichte und Gegenwart.* Erster Band A-C. Tubingen: J.C.A. Mohr (Paul Siebeck), 1957, pp. 1065f) Also see Wilhem & Marion Pauck, *Paul Tillich: His Life & Thought. Vol. 1: Life* (New York: Harper & Row, 1976) pp. 191-192, Tillich, op. cit., 1987, p. 228.

In its 1970 catalog, *Wissenschaftlicke Buchgesellschaft* announces the reprinting of *Berneuchener-Buch* and comments: ". . . Inspired by Paul Tillich, the theologians Ludwig Heitmann, Karl Bernard Ritter and Wilhelm Stahlin produced a book aimed at giving new meanings to all sacred and secular forms of life. A large number of the leaders of German Protestantism personally subscribed at the time to the forward-looking guiding principles (which were laid down in the book). The Berneuchener Buch exercised a decisive influence in the founding and organization of the protestant *Michaelsbruderschaft* (1931)."

Karl Barth in his *Church Dogmatics: The Doctrine of the Word of God, I.1* (translated by G. T. Thompson. Edinburgh: T. & T. Clark,

1936, pp. 68-70) quotes from and criticizes Professor Tillich's comments related to worship, including the Berneuchener position.

I am indebted to Dr. Paul W. Meyer for the Berneuchener references and translation from the German.

6.   In a letter to Thomas Mann in 1943, Professor Tillich "speaks of his own discussions late into the night with his student colleagues, and then he adds, 'What I have become as a theologian, as a philosopher, and as man, I owe in part to the professors (under whom I studied), and in a comparatively overwhelming degree to a student association.'" (James Luther Adams, "Words for Paul Tillich," *Harvard Divinity Bulletin,* January, 1966, 30, 2, p. 9).

7.   Revelation 5:1, 5; 6:1, 3, 5, 7, 9, 12; 7:2; 8:1.

8.   John 3:15, 18-21; 6:50-58; 17:3.

HISTORY AND THEOLOGY[1]

KAIROS AND KAIROI

Question: Dr. Tillich, in your various comments about kairos as the critical point or the fulfillment of time in history, you have said that there is one major kairos -- that is, the Christ event -- but that there are derivative kairoi also at which some decision must be made or some action taken. I wonder if you mean by that, that every decision situation has an element of kairos in it or if this has to do only with certain very important decisive events in history? If the latter is your answer, what would you say are some of the kairoi points in our present world era?

Background of the Term

Dr. Tillich: Another lecture (laughter). That is a very big question. Now let me say how I came to this idea. It was the moment after the breakdown of much in Europe, especially Germany and Austria, in the year 1919.[2] There was a group of people who tried to understand the actual situation as it had developed through the catastrophe of Germany which, somehow, included a catastrophe of the whole world of the nineteenth century. That at least was our feeling. So we said, this is the providential moment within the whole of the present historical situation.

The New Testament

Naturally, then, the New Testament word kairos came to our mind. It is, of course, an old Greek word and meant any moment in which good timing can be done. It has much to do with what you call timing -- finding the right moment to do something which otherwise could not be done. But it is not only the matter of doing, it is also the matter of the situation which makes it possible to do something.

Now this concept of <u>kairos</u> had to be related to what the New Testament calls <u>kairos</u>: namely, the providential moment of the appearance of a new eon, a new period of world development. The New Testament people believed it had happened with the appearance of Jesus whom, for this reason, they called the Christ, the bringer of the New Being. The answer to the relationship of this concept to the experience of our hopes and those of many others in this moment of history was then expressed in such a way that we said, there is the great <u>kairos</u> -- as in Alexandria the religious groups had a festival of the coming of the great eon (they meant the new period of the world). It was called "great" because it was the moment in which the time was fulfilled in a way as never before and never again. So we said, similar experiences happen again and again.

In Germany

Some people felt there was something historically important (not biographically, but historically important) which had happened and out of which a new impulse for action would come. That we called our <u>kairos</u>: but since we kept the criterion of the great <u>kairos</u> over all the other <u>kairoi</u> -- the plural of <u>kairos</u> -- we subjected our <u>kairos</u> to the criterion of the great <u>kairos</u>. This was of fundamental importance, more than we ever imagined when we first used that term: namely, when the Nazis came, they claimed their <u>kairos</u>, too. They even used our terminology in order to say, here is another <u>kairos</u> -- the <u>kairos</u> of the German nation through which all other nations shall be blessed.

Now the criterion, then, of the great <u>kairos</u> -- of Christ -- had to be applied. The analysis was one of the last things I wrote in the German language and for Germany. I wrote a very long article in one of the church magazines about this situation -- about the impossibility of using the term <u>kairos</u> for everything unless it stands under the criterion of the great <u>kairos</u>. From that vantage point --

with the symbol of the cross, especially -- we judged Nazism as a demonic opposition. If the word kairos should be applied at all, we would say a demonic kairos -- a kairos in which a period of destructiveness started. And so it was.

This is the genesis of this term. It has to do with chronos -- the time of the clock -- and must be distinguished as the qualitatively evaluated time and not the quantitatively measured time.

Today

Now if you asked about today, the last thing I said positively about this was in a lecture I gave in Chicago about '47 or '48 -- that means, shortly after the end of the war. There I asked myself your question. And the answer was, there is no positive kairos in the sense of the beginning of a new era. We have nothing with which to begin. We have only a negative kairos, if you want to use that word again -- not demonic but negative -- where silence is the only way to adapt oneself to the situation, because one main character of the situation was the confusion of languages -- the impossibility of finding common symbols, the impossibility of believing that there is a changing point in which great things can be done.

This means that today I do not see any group which makes this claim that a new eon has started in a limited realm or in a larger realm. The feeling of everybody today is much more the negative kairos -- the emptiness which is the symbol of most of the self-confessions of the younger generation. They feel empty, which, then, also is expressed in the existentialist poetry (especially poetry) but also the other arts and philosophy. Now I think this at least partly answers your question.

The Subjective Reception

I may add one thing which otherwise will lead to another question anyhow. It will be pointed out, "So kairos is a subjective concept. You have no objective criteria."

Now this is true. It is as true as it was true that without the prophets the destruction and salvation and later destruction of Jerusalem would not have become a kairos. That means that even Jesus would not have become a kairos without those who received him -- without Peter's confession and all that followed it. Therefore, the only way of dealing with this concept of kairos seems to me to be to accept the fact that it is a subjective-objective structure.

Something happens, but the reception of this something in terms of a turning moment in history -- not only a turning moment on the level of history but a turning point in the fact that something eternal breaks into time and history -- this is the idea of kairos. It is, if you want the arrogant formula, a consciousness to live in a moment where the times must be interpreted with a prophetic spirit. That is what we meant with the term kairos. Now that has answered some of your question.

THE DILEMMA

Question: Dr. Tillich, I want to follow up your answer a little bit in that I wonder how this protects us in any way from either pure subjectivism, on one hand, or from some kind (what I think you criticize in Barth) of complete withdrawal into the realm of the transcendental, on the other? You say, well, always the eternal is judging the world. But if you do not have any specific content of this judgment -- as, for instance, last night you said, "We are not Utopians; we do not foresee any Utopia" -- that seems to me to be one way of saying that we do not have any specific content for this idea of the Kingdom of God or of the demands of Christian ethics in relation to our whole culture. How do you avoid these faults?

Transcendentalism

Dr. Tillich: Now this kairos idea was a way to avoid it, exactly. I mean, it was the only way, I think, we could avoid it. On the other hand, it was not the mere transcendentalism of the Barthians: namely, devaluating history together. That was the one way. This was always done by the Lutheran churches in Germany. They had no valuation of history as something in which something new can happen in a qualitative sense.

So we had to fight with this idea of <u>kairos</u> against the Lutheran churches in Germany, which are practically the German Protestant churches because there are no denominations. (There is a little influence of Calvinism in the West, but that is all. Other denominations do not exist as a manifest power. There are a few hundred thousand, perhaps, related to some American denominations, but otherwise it is all Lutheran.)

The Lutheran attitude was determined, in my opinion, by a misinterpretation of Romans 13: to be "subject" to the authorities which are given by God. Now this interpretation was, in the context of Paul writing to Rome, something very concrete and necessary. It became a universal principal in the Lutheran churches. It had the consequence that they did not try to interfere with history, in any way, to actualize the Kingdom of God in history. It was a purely individualistic-salvation idea. The individual dies and goes to heaven or hell or somewhere. The transformation of history was not taken into consideration. Therefore, there could be no revolution, and so on.[3]

Subjectivism

On the other side, we had the Social Democrats at that time. They were not the majority party but the largest party. They had the greatest influence, for a certain period of five years or a little bit more, on the whole destiny of Germany and Central Europe. Now there we had the opposite. There we had no transcendent foundation at all. Instead of that we were told, "the revolution of the classless society is just around the corner. We, the scientific Socialists, are able to calculate this, because, according to the laws of Marx, it is necessary that under these conditions socialism must come."

Now what came was fascism. The disappointment about this was great, but we had anticipated that. There is no possible belief in Utopia.

THE DEMONIC

So what can be done in the concrete situation -- in the kairos -- is to fight against a special, concrete, particular, demonic power. We saw the demonic power. Demons usually have more than one head, and this demon had two heads. We called the one "capitalism" and the other "nationalism." We believed that the fight against these two heads had to be done in the name of the kairos. Now what capitalism was in Germany (still around 1900) is hard to imagine for Americans who were born only in the last generation. And what nationalism was, then, came out in its full horror in Nazism.

Therefore, we saw the situation just as it was in Germany. We used these two heads of the demonic forces in order to fight against them. That was the whole meaning of this idea. So you see we avoided, on the one hand, Socialist Utopianism, which is the horizontal line and has no vertical line at all, and Lutheran transcendentalism, if you want to call it so, namely, the looking up to the eternal without considering the temporal.

THEONOMY

Question: Dr. Tillich, this is, I can see, a most useful solution to the dilemma. I wonder, does it provide kairos? Does it provide a tool of any kind that the historian can use in looking back at history -- say, the French Revolution -- or must it be in a subjective situation that one has experienced?

Dr. Tillich: It was the latter. It was an experience situation, as all the prophetic figures of the past have also experienced it in themselves. The basis, of course, very often has been their very keen understanding of the actual historical situation. The Jewish prophets knew exactly what happened in the conspiracies of the court or in the service of foreign gods and all that they criticized in the law courts -- the injustice. Now things today which the newspapers relate every day about our country, they also knew, although they often lived in the desert. But with sharp eyes they were able to see what was to be seen. In this sense it is subjective.

Now we can perhaps use kairos as a tool for going back into history. It might help the interpretation of history. And this brings me to the third concept which we had. The first was kairos; we started with that. This concept, as your second question showed, immediately brought us to the concept of the demonic, which I consider to be the second most important concept we used. This concept has become widely used, even by newspaper writers. Then, the third concept which we used was theonomy. Here your question has a bearing on it.

During these years, besides being one of the interpreters of the religious socialist movement, I was also at the University of Berlin and had to give lectures on what the Germans called geistesgeschicthe. A much better word would be spiritual history, but the word "spiritual" is taken away from our language, so we cannot use it. So it is called intellectual history or history of ideas or history of thought, which is all much too intellectualistic. We have no word for spirit. Now, however we call it, I had to lecture about the development of ideas in the Western World. (And I do it again in Harvard now.)

HISTORICAL DEVELOPMENT

There in my lectures at the University of Berlin the following curve developed, probably under the influence of my interpretation of history in connection with the religious socialist movement. It was the curve which we had in the ancient world and had in the Western world in the modern period.

Archaic Period

It starts with an archaic period which is theonomous -- meaning, that in it the forms of life and thought are in the atmosphere of the ultimate, of the holy, of the divine, of religion, if you want to call it so. There is no real separation of the religious and the cultural.

Critical Period

Then comes the beginning criticism which the early philosophers started and Socrates brought to fulfillment over the Sophists.

After the critical period, a classical period appears in which the archaic tradition was still preserved. It was not yet wasted away, but it was already put into rational forms -- the classical arts, on the one hand, and people like Socrates and Plato, on the other hand.

Classical Period

I think the real classical moment in the Greek history of thought is the middle dialogues of Plato. There you still have the full substance of the mythological age and you already have the highest application of rationality. A little bit earlier in the Periclean Age we have the great classical art. Now this is the one thing.

A New Archaic Period

Then, more and more, this classical art wastes away the religious substance, which still is preserved in it, and becomes naturalistic. You can see the naturalistic art in full development in the museum of Naples. Then the reaction begins. With the wasting away of the religious substance -- namely, of the leading symbols of the ultimate -- an emptiness occurs. This emptiness then is filled -- in Greek development where it is very clear -- by religious groups. The Platonic School was always religious and became fully [religiously] conscious in the Neo-Platonic development. The later Stoics became religious. The Neo-Pythagoreans were religious. Even Aristotle was used for the scheme of the Alexandrian kind of thinking which, then, was used by Christian theologians as their basic theological structure.[4]

Now all this is a curve from the archaic to a new archaic period. This new archaic period you can see in the art of the tomb stones, of the stone coffins or sarcophagi. You can see it in the catacombs and later on in the early Christian mosaics. So we have another theonomy.

CONTEMPORARY APPLICATION

Now the idea was, are we not, perhaps, today in such a situation?

All these periods have occurred: the early medieval period as the fullest expression of the Western archaism or archaic period; then the development of the Renaissance; the late Gothic period; the late nominalistic period developed toward the Renaissance where we have a classical period in some nations. (For instance, the classical period in Germany was much later. It was after Kant in the beginning of the nineteenth century.) The Western nations were early in their development of a classical period. In any case, there slowly developed out of this a period of naturalism and of emptiness. We are in a reaction against this. It is the religious resurgence, as it has been called. However bad that resurgence may be in its concrete utterances, it expresses, at least, the desire for a new filling of the emptiness with substance coming from the ultimate. This I would call theonomy.

Religious Socialism

What we developed in the religious socialist context was possibilities of a coming theonomy. It had very little to do with the petty bourgeois type of German socialism which, of course, could not resist the tremendous bohemian and aristocratic attack of Nazism, but which even today is not able to take over the leadership. This was not our religious socialism. Ours was a view of a completely new period of history or, as we often called it, a new theonomy.

The critical period is autonomy. The period against the critical -- the authoritarian period in the church -- is heteronomy. Theonomy is a period in which the autonomous forms of life are filled with the ultimate substance. Now that was our idea.

So, we had a key for the interpretation of history, at least of Western history. When I still look back at what that meant for my understanding of history and for the understanding of many generations of students to whom I tried to give this, [I realize that] they now think largely in these terms about Western history and about the problems of a new theonomy. Now that is my answer to your question.

A Cyclical Interpretation

Question: This is a cyclical interpretation then?

Dr. Tillich: It was so in Greece. It was so again in the medieval period. It might be cyclical, generally, although it is hard to say this because the Greeks were a small section. But then it spread over the whole ancient culture, which completely disappeared. Then there was the Middle Ages. And now [the historical development] is in another place. It is not in the same place. The Greeks as Greeks, in the old sense, have disappeared. The [conception of the] whole reality is another one. So it did not return to the same place where it had developed. But the great development -- the new development -- was then another realm in which the cycle is going on. Yes, that is right. It is cyclical.

Non-Western Cultures

Question: This is really Western civilization you are dealing with. By excluding the rest of the world histories, does this qualify the thesis, the interpretation?

Dr. Tillich: Yes, now this is a question I expected. I am glad you ask it. At that time we lived in European provincialism. We did not think very much of the Asiatic cultures, which already have their cycles. I do not know what I should say.

The difference seems to me (as far as I can see from my knowledge of India, which is book knowledge, and from my meeting of Japan,[5] which is more existential knowledge) that they never came to a point in which the autonomy -- the autonomous reason -- was as developed as it was in the Western world. I think that this is the difference. However, there was always a tendency toward autonomy in India. The Kshatriya[6] -- the knights of the aristocratic class -- was an autonomous force in a certain time, the time of the Upanishads and so was comparatively able to develop things of their own. But the Brahman caste was always the superior one, and it is still so up to today. Therefore, the full autonomy -- the full liberation from the hteronomous effects of religion -- did not occur on Asiatic soil, as far as I can see with my limited knowledge. This would mean that it was a limited circle, yet it was also a circle. I mean we have in India a continuous action and reaction. But it is not such a definite and clear circle. Neither it is in Japan.

Now the question will be: what will happen if the Japanese culture now receives the Western influence, which it does? In every minute of every day something new happens in Japan in this respect. The old disappears. Whether this will lead, as it already has in the younger generation, to emptiness (I use that as a general covering word) and despair, and even schizophrenia (as the Japanese people told me, "We are a schizophrenic nation"), and whether similar developments may be ahead under the influence of the radical autonomy of Western thinking if it enters Asia are real questions.

CHRISTIANITY AND OTHER WORLD RELIGIONS

Comment: You have partly touched on the question I was going to ask a little while ago. It is true that up to the present time Western history has been pretty limited and parochial, has it not? (Yes) Now it is beginning to discover that the West is not the world. All over the West we are having Asian studies programs. You have said in a number of your books that one of the problems we have to face now is to discover the relation of our Christianity to these other religions of the world. You have indicated there are creative factors in all history. The question I would like to ask is: have other peoples, have other religious groups, discovered Christ, to some extent, even though unheard of, using a different terminology and so on? Would you go a little farther along that line?

Encounter with Islam and Buddhism

Dr. Tillich: Now this requires two lectures: one about the encounter of the world religions within themselves and the other about the encounter of the world religions with secularism. These are two different subject matters; each of them is extremely important for our situation.[7]

Question: Would you just indicate the trend of your thinking along these lines?

Dr. Tillich: First of all, I believe that today there is comparatively little influence from one religion to the other. There is, of course, missionary activity in Japan and in India. The South Indian Church is quite important in the whole picture. Even so, I do not think that a real conversion to Christianity of the main Buddhist line is possible in any foreseeable time.

IN AFRICA

Everywhere it is quite possible to convert the masses of those who have never had a developed religion. Then the Christian culture, together with the Christian religion, has influence, for instance in the masses of India, and especially in Africa.

But Africa is not the primary problem in the encounter of the world religions. The Africans are not able, perhaps not even willing to maintain their traditional religions. They now have three religions in competition; Christianity, which is not the most effective; Islam, which up to now is by far the most effective (it always was in Africa and always barred Christianity from any missionary influence by a big barrier of northern Africa); and communism. We do not know which of these three will conquer Africa. That is an open question and prophecy in the sense of foreseeing is not very useful.

IN ASIA

The other aspect is the encounter, for instance, with Buddhism in Asia. Now I only know Japanese Buddhism, which is a different form from the original Buddhism which went through China and was transformed there.[8] It had more elements of concretization -- of a relation to the concrete reality -- in it. Zen Buddhism is something else.[9] It is not the same as the original Buddhism or as Mahayana Buddhism.[10] Both Hinduism and Buddhism have very dynamic missions here in America now.

The Zen Buddhist mission is a very ambiguous thing. The people who take it, most of them, want to take it without "sitting"[11] for two years. This process means going through a hell which is even worse than the hell of a successful psychoanalysis. Without this sacrifice it is, of course, impossible for them to get what is really meant in this language. If you do not experience enlightenment[12] -- and I saw this -- you cannot really judge it. We who have never made the meditations and performed the bodily discipline which is necessary are unable to have a deeper understanding of what is going on there. Therefore, the superficial mission that is now going on here and in Europe, especially in connection with psychotherapy, is often so superficial.

I talked about it with some of the Zen masters, for instance. and asked them, "Won't your really great thing be presented here as a fashion of Park Avenue, New York?" They said to my astonishment, "Yes, we want to present it because we believe that even if it is as distorted as it is in the reception by this type of fashion-seeker, there is always a little bit of the truth in it." They said that when Christianity came to the barbarian Germanic tribes, they did not understand the depths of Augustine or Paul, but they took something. Then, out of the something, later on -- in hundreds of years -- more developed. Therefore, they do this kind of missionary work. They did not accept my warning in this respect at all. I spoke for them, not against them, but they did not accept it.

CRITICISM OF BUDDHISM

They better accepted my criticism of their technology. It has no real motive for (1) social action, (2) for an understanding of history or, (3) for valuation of the individual personality. These three criticism were very severely discussed in my conversations with them. So the final result, I would say, perhaps, is that with respect to the idea of God -- of the ultimate, even of what they call the Buddha spirit, the Spiritual power with a capital S as I like to call it -- there is something present in the great religions which has revelatory and saving force. I do not doubt this at all.

On the other hand, when we apply the criterion of agape -- of love -- then these three things are lacking. There is not this form of agape. There is a tremendous amount of compassion.[13] The life we had there was wonderful, just for this reason. But it was different from agape. The Christian concept of agape, of love in the New Testament sense, is something else. It implies the transformation of individuals and the transformation of reality. It does not demand the formless self as is the case in Buddhism, but it demands the fulfilled self. In the Christian doctrine, individuality has ultimate meaning. Here they must take something from us.

We can take something from them. It is a help in overcoming our primitivism with religious symbols, of which they have a much deeper understanding. I often felt that they must think -- even as Christian theologians, of course, think -- that what is going on in the missionary churches is, for them, almost childish. They feel tremendous superiority in this respect -- the not demythologized symbolism of the Christian churches. I believe that here we can understand much from what they give us.

Now that is only a small section of the encounter of the world religions in relation to the primitive areas where missions are going on from these three sides. Islam is in the forefront now. The other aspect is the encounter of Christianity with probably the highest non-Christian religion (at least in terms of basically mystical religion), namely, Buddhism.

I cannot answer the question of Christianity's encounter with Islam. Islam was, is, and probably always will be, a riddle for me which I cannot approach. I have made all kinds of attempts to understand why it has this power, although it is in a very minor consequence the result of some Christian and some Jewish ideas. The way in which the people live according to the Prophet's law is something astonishing and in itself great, although it is on an infinitely more primitive level than Judaism, Christianity, Buddhism and others.

Question: Would it not be true that the more advanced cultural Hindus and Buddhists would not admit that we are superior to them in the realm of love? Do they not often claim that they really have emphasized love and compassion? I have heard some of them say that we need to gain some of their insight or we of the West will destroy ourselves very quickly.

Dr. Tillich: Yes, now they have more compassion. I mean, the way in which they treat you shows that they have a great power of identifying themselves with somebody else. This is certainly the case. But they have no desire to offer revolutionary transformation of religion. They have no real reformation in this sense, which refers to the masses of the people. Zen believes it is a reformation. Shin[14] believes it is a reformation. But that is in the upper classes; that is not general. The reformation which is related to the general situation -- to the masses of the people -- they do not have. The political transformation based on the idea of justice they do not have either.

Encounter with Communism

Question: Would you make a few comments about the encounter of Christianity and communism as religious groups?

Dr. Tillich: Perhaps you mean in Russia?

Comment: You spoke of the revolution in Africa and other places with communism, Islam, and Christianity. Now there must be a religious and theological encounter there. How do you view this?

IN AFRICA

Dr. Tillich: Now in Africa the situation is comparatively clear. The question -- no, let me put it this way -- the competition between communism and Islam is very strong because Islam has the social-ethical pathos itself. Therefore, Pakistan is much more anti-Russian than India, although many other conditions are very similar. The poverty is everything. But I think that Pakistan and the other Arabian nations are anti-communist.

The Arabs are aristocratic. They have some social and juristic rules which are primitive enough to be fulfilled. The fulfillment of the five prayers of the pilgrimage to Mecca[15] and of other rules such as family life, drinking, eating and all of this, is something these tribes can take. If you want to speak to them about the forgiveness of sins or about the Christ bringing a new reality or the question of salvation generally, then this would not fit them. The freedom of the children of God, of which Paul speaks, is not acceptable to their situation. They are still under the law.

The law is not broken through on Islamic soil except in some Persian groups where there is the sophitic mysticism. There we have something which breaks through the law. I believe there is some very great mysticism there, but that is the only point.

For the African tribes, I believe it is clear that: Islam is first of all a transcendent monotheism, which is Jewish in character; then there are the prayers to Him in regular intervals; and then there is the life ordered by the Koran and interpreted by the religions leaders in all centuries, that is enough for them. But the paradox of the Christian idea of salvation, of forgiveness, of justification by faith, and all these are too strange to them.

Also the Christian identification with Western culture in all these missionary enterprises is something that is extremely dangerous for Christianity. I think they wrongly introduce ways of life which are good in America (or at least half good in America) and which suddenly are not good in other countries.

When I talked with missionaries in Japan, there was the same situation. I always told them, "Do not introduce American Baptistism or Lutheranism or Episcopalianism into this country. These differences and the ethical attitudes in all respect (which also are different here in this country) are not the real problem for them." So they do not have much success. Less than 1% are Christian in Japan in a people of ninety million. This is the situation there.

IN RUSSIA

With communism we have the great encounter in Russia. There something has repeated itself in my opinion. We find a completely sacramentalized religion (as the Greek Orthodox Church was) in which the prophetic spirit was prohibited completely, even more radically than in the Roman Church, and which fell into innumerable forms of superstition. It had no power to resist an historical ethical religion which Islam was. Therefore, Islam conquered the Eastern half of Christianity. In the same way communism in its origin and message is a secularized prophetism. The classless society is another word for the kingdom of God, namely, the place where justice will prevail. That is the original meaning of this communist message. Again a non-Christian religion was able to overrun Russia because of this sacramentalized religion.

So we have here the same thing. Communism is secular in its attack. Now in Russia it is something else. But in its original attack -- in Marx' prophetic style in the Communist Manifesto and so on -- it is a social-ethical religion in contrast to a mystical-ritual religion as the Eastern Church was. Therefore, it again prevailed against another wing of the Eastern Church. Now that is one of the ways in which communism encountered religion.

I do not think that in the West where communism was born -- Marx, after all, was a German Jew -- the influence will be too great. There the social-ethical point of view is given by our dependence upon the Old Testament. That tradition is perhaps, for a long time, strong enough to prevent an invasion of communism. But this is a decisive question.

FOOTNOTES

1.   Originally published in *Foundations: A Baptist Journal of History and Theology,* Vol. XIV, No. 3, July-September 1971, pp. 209-223.

2.   In his Rauschenbush lecture at Colgate Rochester Divinity School, March 30, 1958, he stated, "Decisive for the development of my thoughts and that of my group was the situation in Germany when we returned from the First World War. Imperial Germany and royal Prussia had come to an end. Social Democrats, in cooperation with the Catholic Center Party, had taken over the German Republic and defended it in the beginning successfully against attacks from left and right. Protestant churches, traditionally aligned with an aristocratic and paternalistic conservatism, stood aside. Rejecting the revolution and its consequences, they tried to find an emergency solution to the problems which arose from the separation of church and state. The estrangement between the predominantly Lutheran Church and Socialist labor movement -- the split was extremely radical in Imperial Germany -- underwent little change in the Republic. In this situation we searched for the ultimate roots of this bitter conflict between the churches and the Socialist movement." ("Beyond Utopianism and

Escape From History." Colgate Rochester Divinity School *Bulletin*, Vol. XXXI, May, 1959, No. 2, pp. 32-40)

3.   Tillich had elaborated on this point in his Rauschenbusch lecture: "Partly under the influence of Luther's doctrine of the two realms, the earthly and the spiritual, the churches preached judgment and salvation of the individual beyond history, in the transcendent Kingdom of God. [Humanity's] historical existence is determined by [the] state of sin. Political power has the function of restraining sin by threat of severe punishment. To be sure, the representatives of the political power are, along with all their subjects, in the same state of estrangement. Luther never doubted this. Therefore they will abuse their power. But even bad authorities are better than no authorities at all. Therefore they cannot be resisted or attacked. Attempts to change them, except through prayer, are against the divine will. There is no justification whatsoever for revolutions." ("Beyond Utopianism ..." op. cit.)

4.   In contract to Antioch, the Alexandrian approach was a more or less uniform procedure in exegesis of the Scriptures that consisted of a nonhistorical, nonliteral seeking of what was regarded as more profound, mystical, and spiritual. It is still termed typological or allegorical. Outstanding thinkers were Clement and Origen who were intent on presenting Christianity to the cultivated and wanted to show that Christ was the summit of all human knowledge. (*New Catholic Encyclopedia,* Vol. 1, New York: McGraw-Hill, 1967, pp. 304-305)

5.   Tillich visited Japan in May, June and July 1960. He discussed some of its significance for him in his conversations with the psychotherapists.

6.   The doctrine of the fourfold classes of Hindu society comes from the hymn of the Rigveda that describes the primeval sacrifice from which the world was created. "From the head of the primeval man appeared the Brahman, from his arms the warrior (Kshatriya), from his trunk the class of merchants and craftsman

(Vaishya) and from his feet the menial (Shudra)." (*Encyclopedia Britannica*, Vol. 11. Chicago: William Benton, 1966, p. 511)

"Tradition says that the original Kshatriya, created from the arms of the deity and given the gift of strength to protect treasure and life so that order could prevail, were destroyed by Parasurama, the sixth reincarnation of Vishnu, as a punishment for their tyranny. The legend probably embodies the story of the long struggle for supremacy between priests and rulers, which ended in victory for the former. By the end of the Vedic era the Brahmans were supreme, the Kshatriya had been relegated to second place." (Ibid., Vol. 13, p. 500)

7.   In *Christianity and the Encounter of the World Religions* (New York: Columbia University Press, 1963) Tillich elaborated the development that occurred in this discussion.

8.   See footnotes 10 and 11 in "The Experiential, The Theological and Psychotherapy" in this volume.

9.   Zen Buddhism is one of the principle sects (shū) of Buddhism in Japan. It disavows abstraction, generalization, explanation, argument. Instead it appeals directly to facts of personal experience without any intermediary. The Four Great Statements of Zen sum up what is claimed by Zen as religion:

> "A special transmission outside the Scriptures;
> No dependence upon words and letters;
> Direct pointing to the soul of man [sic];
> Seeing into one's nature and the attainment
> of Buddhahood."

Because the answer is found where the question is raised, followers are urged to find within themselves the answer to any question raised from within themselves. Out of the dialectical and apparently nonsensical talk between master and seeker comes insight into the nature of one's being. Such enlightenment requires the full attention and force of the personality.

"To the question, 'What is Zen?' a master gave this answer, 'Boiling oil over a blasting fire.' This scorching experience we have to go through before Zen smiles on us and says, 'Here is your home.'" (D. T. Suzuki, *Zen Buddhism:* selected writings. Edited by William Barrett. Garden City, New York: Doubleday Anchor Books, 1956, pp. 3-24)

10. Along with Theravada, Mahayana is one of the two major schools of Buddhism. By means of its cardinal doctrine it teaches the broad path to salvation. That is, "all sentient beings possess the Buddha-nature and hence are capable of attaining enlightenment." This aspect, followed in Tibet, China, and Japan, probably developed in the two centuries before Christ, "with its starting point very likely furnished by the speculations on the nature of the Buddha development by the Mahasanghikas, a group of dissent monks who broke away from the orthodox community at the second great Buddhist council c. 383 b.c. According to this school, the Buddha was no longer a human teacher but a lokottara or supramundane being who appeared on earth in an apparitional form as Sakyamuni." Faith and devotion to the Buddha plus love and compassion for all creatures are stressed. (*Encyclopedia Britannica*, op.cit., vol. 14, p. 631)

11. Technically, "to sit" means to sit cross-legged in meditation. It refers to a motionless sitting and some sort of concentration or peaceful attention to the object without straining to achieve effects. Usually the legs are crossed, the back straining, the breathing regular, and the eyes only slightly open. (Ernest Wood, *Zen Dictionary*. New York: Philosophical Library, 1962, p. 157)

12. Enlightenment is a constantly experienced state of satori or a getting beyond concepts. It is an added mode of experience similar to the opening of a third eye. "Satori may be defined as an intuitive looking into the nature of things in contradistinction to the analytical or logical understanding of it. Practically, it means the unfolding of a new world hitherto unperceived in the con-

fusion of a dualistically-trained mind." (Suzuki, op. cit., pp. 83-108).

13.   As a religion, Buddhism has given the world two major values: (1) "the idea of personal discipline to gain freedom from craving in the ultimate tranquility in Nirvana"; and (2) "the idea of unselfish devotion to the good of others for the sake of their deliverance from ill." (Clarence H. Hamilton, *Buddhism: A Religion of Infinite Compassion:* Selections from Buddhist Literature. Edited, with an Introduction and Notes. New York: The Liberal Arts Press, 1952, p. xxiii) The second of the four states in cultivating the unlimited emotions is compassion. It requires concentrating on the sufferings of others in order to suffer with them, and thereby desire to remove their suffering. With Mahayanists compassion achieved a rank of importance equal with wisdom. (Edward Donze, *Buddhism: Its Essence and Development.* Oxford, England: Bruno Cassirer, 1957, pp. 102, 128)

14.   See Footnote 4 in "The Experiential, The Theological and Psychotherapy" in this volume. The True Pure Land Sect is based upon the 18th vow: "Having heard the name of Amida, they rejoice and trust in him with the whole heart." This vow is the most liberal of Buddhist vows, "providing as it does for universal salvation by the power of Amida Buddha, who will take all [people] who have faith in him to the original and eternal paradise. . . . By it, Amida fulfills all religious and moral obligations for those who fully trust in him." For this group, neither the repetition of Amida's name nor the practice of virtue are conditions for salvation. "The essence of the True Sect is that the power of faith proceeds from the original vow. The repetition of Amida's name is a revelation of [a person's] faith." (Robert C. Armstrong, *An Introduction to Japanese Buddhist Sects.* Canada: Privately Printed for Mrs. Robert Cornell Armstrong, 1950, pp. 211-217)

15.   The obligatory worship of God in Islam consists of five daily prayers preceded by necessary ablution in accord with the practice of the Prophet: before sunrise, just after noon, in the late after-

noon, immediately after sunset, and about two hours later. (*Encyclopedia Britannica,* op. cit., vol. 12, p. 663)

PSYCHOLOGY AND THEOLOGY[1]

INTRODUCTION

For this particular hour we are going to concentrate our questions on the general area of psychology. In the last hour we saw that history merged over into psychoanalysis, Zen Buddhism, and their interrelationships; but we will try to focus, if we can, primarily on the relationship of theology and the discipline of psychology in its various dimensions.

Dr. Tillich: "Ism" I must make a statement before any question. I used the world "nationalism." And in a short talk outside [during the break] I was again reminded of the fact that "ism" in English is not what ismus is in German. Both are derived from the Greek syllable ismos. In English, "ism" can be something good. In German, every "ism" is a negation -- is a distorted -- of something. So when I said "nationalism," I did not mean national self-consciousness or valuation of the nation or support of the nation, even in a sacrificial way. But it meant: making nation the god -- the ultimate concern. And, of course, when I used the word in this sense, then the question had to come: Isn't nationalism in the sense in which it is usually understood something good which may become bad?

So, please excuse this semantic difficulty, which I see in many things. For instance, to come to this word "psychologism." Psychology is good. Psychologism is bad. Now you continue.

FREEDOM AND DESTINY

Question: What do you mean by freedom and destiny as a description of the determining and creating powers or activities of [human beings]?

Dr. Tillich: Now what do I mean? Do you mean that I shall define the two terms?

Question: Yes. In what sense is [humanity] free?

Dr. Tillich: Yes. I will not repeat my statement (good natured chuckle). No finite being is absolutely free. Every finite being is in [its] being embedded in that which is given to [it]: namely, [one's] parents, the heritage of them, the place in which [one] is born, the time in which [one] is born, [one's] surroundings, day by day. But there is another element. I call all this [one's] destiny. And this destiny is given to [one]. You can also call it fate, but fate has a negativistic connotation from the Latin fatum, which was a dark power, while destiny is a meaningful power. It has to do with the Christian symbol of providence. In any case, everybody is in this concrete situation and cannot escape it.

Now there are, however, possibilities of reacting to all these elements within ourselves and outside of ourselves in terms of a centered reaction. A centered reaction which goes through deliberation and decision, which everybody can feel in [oneself] is something else. This is what I would call freedom.

Now the question is whether the destiny, for instance, our psychological constitution, is preventing freedom? I would say we cannot say this, because if we say it, we contradict ourselves in claiming that it is true. The concept of a true statement and a false statement is based on the fact that we are free to decide in our argument, following something which is not our destiny but which are the rules of logic which transcend our personal destiny.

We are free in so far as we are able to center all elements which are given in us by our destiny in one center, which we call our ego or ourself. These words are all very ambiguous. Let us call it our centered self. In this centered self, then, we deliberate and we decide. This act of deliberation and decision -- or in other terminology the reaction to a stimulus -- in terms of our centered self is what I would define as freedom. Freedom is not the popular discussion of determinism and indeterminism, so called freedom of the will. Our freedom is our total reaction and, therefore, not only our will but "we" are free. And "we" includes all the dimensions of our being. It includes every cell of our body, as we know, of our brain and of our own existence.

So these are the two concepts. Now they are continuously intermixed. Nobody is free beyond the margin which [one's] destiny leaves [one]. This margin is not very large, but it is continuously present, which makes it possible for us to be creative.

[People] have creative freedom. That is another element in it. Creation is a word which is originally used for God; but since what we use for God must have some analogy in us, we also experience creative moments. In creative moments we transcend the given, that which is given in us in this moment. this transcending the given happens in a centered reaction. And this centered reaction, then, is freedom.

So you have now a preliminary definition of the two concepts -- a definition which can appeal to immediate self-awareness. We all know that this is a way in which we discuss here in this hour, in this place: we reflect; we considerate; we use norms of experience, of experiential material, of logical consistency, and so on. We go beyond our merely psychological reaction into which we fall, when, for instance we are intoxicated or half-asleep or our totality is not centered any more or it is disrupted into two different centers. All this happens all the time, but sometimes we act in a centered way. Then the destiny element in us is trespassed by the centered reaction of a centered self. That makes creation possible, and that is what I would call freedom.

Anxiety: Destructive and Constructive

Question: Dr. Tillich, many psychologists seem to take the position that anxiety is an abnormal condition and that it is a generating factor in neurosis. Then, another position seems to be that anxiety is a universal condition of [humanity] and that it is essential to [one's] growth and development. Now if there are two kinds of anxiety, one that is productive of neurosis and one that leads to growth, how can these two be distinguished? Can they be distinguished phenomenologically or are there objective ways to distinguish them?

Dr. Tillich: I think that there are objective ways in which we can distinguish them. Of course, I do not believe that anxiety can be analyzed away because I do not believe that death can be analyzed away. That means our finitude. It is not an object to be analyzed away. In this sense, I would say, this not distinguishing neurotic anxiety from existential anxiety is a very short-sighted way of thinking about [humanity]. [Humanity's] anxiety is identical with the awareness of [one's] having-to-die: of [one's] coming-from-nothing and [one's] going-to-nothing, of [one's] being threatened in every moment by the contingencies of reality (sickness and accident and everything) and the anxiety connected with this.

I never have seen a human being in any culture -- even the Asiatic cultures -- where there is not the desire to escape death and the anxiety of not being able to escape death. Otherwise, no war would be possible and no criminal justice would be possible. Punishment of death would not mean anything for people, but even in Asia it means something. So, everybody has a desire to live, a natural self-affirmation of [one's] life, and wants to preserve it and increase it. It is always both. The existential anxiety is identical with the finitude of every finite being. Of course, in this animals and [people] are on equal footing because they are also anxious to preserve themselves and to escape dangers.

Now the neurotic anxiety appears when we are not able to face the concrete occasions of anxiety with courage. In my book, *The Courage To Be*, that was my criterion. I believe that is still the case. Neurotic people can be defined, perhaps, as people who cannot stand the view of reality as it really is. They have not the courage to face it, courage which comes from all kinds of sources, vital as well as religious sources. Therefore, they withdraw into a limited position and defend this limited position with all their strength -- the so-called defense mechanisms, which are not altogether bad. Because if you break them down, which often can be done in psychoanalysis, you may put a human being before the whole of reality, a human being who is not able to actually face it. Therefore, the removal of all defense mechanisms might become a catastrophic thing for somebody instead of being a way of opening up.

It is the wisdom of the analyst, psychotherapist or the counselor, to break down the compulsions. If [one] does it, [one] must know that maybe this was the way in which this weak nature could save itself from breaking down, by accepting these compulsive reductions of freedom. Here we come again to the problem of freedom. The ideal, of course, of the analysis is to break them down in order to set the person free from the destiny in which these elements of compulsion have developed. This, I believe, is about what I could say.

So the criterion seems to me to be: can you face reality or can you not? Perhaps we all have some neurotic elements, some places where we cannot face reality. I think, if we think about ourselves, there are places where we simply escape or go into a castle which is then protected by our defense mechanisms.

There are similar examples in religion. For the minister it is very difficult whether and to what degree [one] can break down the compulsions which are connected with a superstitious sticking to literalism or other things. The break-down of the fundamentalistic self-certainty would be an example. This self-certainty is a mass neurotic phenomenon -- not in itself, but in the moment in which people see and know in some part of their being that their stubbornness is wrong and that the truth is here on the other side, the critical side, for instance, with respect to Bible. They cannot stand it; so they repress it; so they are compulsively bound to their orthodoxy; so they must become fanatic because they have to repress their own doubts.

Now that is a phenomenon which is very analogous to the general phenomenon of neurosis -- the necessity of living on a limited level -- not to face reality as a whole. There are places where we cannot face reality as a whole, and that is the element of neurosis in all of us. Now that would be my distinction.

Gestalt Psychology and Human Experience

Question: Professor Tillich, would you have any comments on Gestalt psychology in so far as it provides theoretical descriptions of particular significant aspects of human experience?

Dr. Tillich: Yes, now I could, for instance, say that one whole part of my philosophy of life is the function of centeredness, of integration and the continuous fight with disintegration. This, I think, is best seen from the theory of Gestalt. I believe that this can make understandable the phenomenon which I described to the first question as the phenomenon of freedom. I do not know how you can have freedom without centeredness. If we are not centered, if we are parts, then we cannot be free -- because then now the one part, now the other part, takes over. In real schizophrenic cases, parts take over so much that the centeredness is taken away.

So I would say that if you would identify centeredness with gestalt, in the sense of this theory, then for our special purpose now, Gestalt theory is extremely important in order to understand freedom. You cannot understand it otherwise.

But you cannot understand spontaneity in the animal realm, and partly in the realm of vegetative life either, without gestalt. Every plant or every animal is a living gestalt before you can analyze the inorganic and chemical processes which are going on in it. They are not the priors, but the priors are always the gestalt. And then we can say, in this gestalt -- some processes are going on.

Bodily health means that none of the processes of the body, which keep it alive in every moment, takes over and excludes others. So here again health and centeredness are the same. Even the old

Greek medical people knew this; the preponderance of a Pythagorean[2] set, one number, which means one power of being, produces disharmony; or in the Ionian philosophy of medicine[3] the taking over of one substance produces disharmony; and we have the same in Heraclitus,[4] who says that if we have too much of the watery substance and not enough of the fiery substance, then we must become sick and die.

All these ideas show that only as long as the elements are subjected to a center which is not identical with any of the elements, only then, we are healthy and we are able to act. Now if this is Gestalt theory, I would believe that Gestalt theory is an element of every doctrine of freedom and spontaneity.

THE NEW BEING AND THERAPEUTIC PROCESSES

Question: Dr. Tillich, the question I ask, I think, is related to the first three answers you have given. What is the relationship between the New Being and the process that takes place between two individuals that we call therapeutic, whether or not either of the individuals stands consciously in the context of the Christian faith or is aware of the process which you identify as the reality of the New Being?

Dr. Tillich: Yes, now this is actually the question of medical healing, in this case psychotherapeutic healing and religious healing.

Now first of all, I reject the term "faith healing" because it has connotations of mere magic. Although I know that there are magical elements even in our conversation now, they never can be removed fully -- namely, the effect of something unconscious in me or something unconscious in you, which is going on all the time. Nevertheless, faith healing, in the way in which it is treated, is conscious magic; it is not magic which is fluidity between people, which is always there. This conscious magic has nothing to do with religious healing.

Now let's go into the boundary line between them. I believe that psychotherapeutic or psychoanalytic healing has to be done in cases where -- either with or without bodily symptoms -- a centered being, a [person] as a centered being, disintegrates. Elements become unruly and take over. This is, then, a state of neurosis or psychosis or the forms of psychotic illnesses and the lesser form of neurotic illnesses. They are all related to the center. They have become a kind of independent development in the psychological realm, therefore, mental disease. It is the same as independent development in the bodily realm on the basis of decentralization or disintegration. This can be healed.

Let's suppose a successful medical healing or a successful psychotherapeutic healing occurs. Both are possible. Then the question arises: after the compulsory elements are reduced, or even removed to a great extent, [a person] has become free now; what is to be done with [one's] freedom? There the answer cannot be given by the psychoanalyst as psychoanalyst. It can, perhaps, be given by [one] as a personality of a religious character. [One] may be a priest, I mean, to the other one; and in Protestantism everyone can be a priest to the other one. that might be, but then [one] is not doctor; [one] is not healer in the psychotherapeutic sense. The same can happen at the sick bed with a doctor, who can be a priest at the same time [one] gives [one's] drugs and [one's] orders how to behave.

In principle the two functions are distinguished. The religious function appeals to the center of the personality to actualize an ultimate concern. Here the question of the separate functions arises. Everybody who has no ultimate concern has no center above [oneself] for [one's] own center, in which the center can rest. [One] is in some way spiritually sick. And we all are. We do not call that sickness; we usually call it sin or estrangement. Here it is impossible that the medical approach, as such, can heal. Here the experience of ultimacy comes in, which is not opposite to the medical problem but is in it, although it is something different. So I would say that the two forms of healing are different.

A healing of the whole [person] is possible only if all sides are taken care of. There are four of them at least:

the ultimate, which, I would say, is the matter of ultimate concern, is the ultimate center in which our center can rest;

the psychological, which is often connected with the first, but not always;

the bodily, which is often connected with the two first, but not always;

and then the sociological healing, which is always necessary because otherwise, if in the social existence a [person] becomes necessarily sick again after [one] has been healed in psychotherapy, something is wrong which also must be healed.

Therefore, we have these four healers in the history of [humankind]. We have the priest. We have the psychological helper, mostly in our period which has come to full self-consciousness. We have the medical healer. We have the people who do social healing. And it is interesting that the word "savior," the Greek soter, was applied to all of these groups. Asclepius was a savior. The princes in the period after Alexander the Great were called in Greek sotorus, because they healed the estrangement of the society from its true being. They all belong together.

You cannot separate them, but you also should not confuse them. No individual medical doctor should claim that if [one] has restored the bodily health of somebody, [that person] is healed. There may be -- just because of this healing -- a development of a psychotherapeutic problem or a religious problem. Nor should anyone say that if somebody is pious or is, let's say in order with God, in the right relationship to the ultimate center, then [one] is healed bodily. This is the mistake of movements like Christian Scientists, who believe that. Nor should anyone say that if somebody is healed psychotherapeutically, [one] is healed with respect to [one's] body and with respect to [one's] religious life. Nor, finally, should a social healer claim, as the Marxist's did, that if only the social situation is in order, then there will be no more sickness and no more anti-ethical acting in any realm.

Now, each one is as foolish as the other. Each of them has its independent function, but each of them has tried to heal the whole [person] as from one point of view. Only by collaboration can they reach the whole [person]. That seems to me to be the situation.

The Status of the Soul

Question: For some time psychology seems to have turned away from the concept of an immaterial, immortal soul and concerned itself with conditions of living and with behavior. As a general position, would you think it is gain or a loss that psychology has turned away from the concept of an immaterial soul and occupied itself with more actual conditions of living?

Dr. Tillich: Yes, now from the scientific point of view the so-called immortal soul had to be dismissed, in any case. It has been dismissed so fully in all scientific discussion since the English empiricists, since the eighteenth century, that in the English language the word "soul" can be used only with great care and then only in poems and, perhaps, in sermons where it is still admissable. In any serious research the word is completely gone. The word is preserved in the word psychology itself -- namely, psyche is the Greek word for "soul," but the English word is forbidden. The Greek is so mysterious anyhow it does not mean much.

Now, I think from the point of view of a scientific approach, it is an advantage that this so-called immortal soul has disappeared, which was a substance beside other substances. I think that since Kant's criticism of the idea of the soul-substance -- and Hume, of course, preceded him in this -- there is no reason to reestablish this in any science. I do not think it is a loss. I think it is a gain.

The loss of the concept "soul" is also a gain theologically because Christianity did not originally teach the doctrine of the immortality of the soul. This is a Platonic formula. It does not mean what it means today in American funeral superstition, but it means something quite different. It means the fact that the essence of a being coming from the world of essences -- or belonging essentially to it, although actually staying in time and space -- is not ultimately hurt by time and space, but is able to have its essential nature eternally. This Platonic doctrine has been accepted by many Christian thinkers, I think with great difficulty, because the Christian symbol is resurrection. That means the whole personality, including the bodily, has an essence and belongs to the essence. But that is a far reaching question.

Now it is necessary to remove this kind of object because it cannot be verified and because you can describe [humanity's] psychological reality without it. If you do describe [humanity's] psychological reality with it, the relationship of the soul to the body becomes completely un-understandable. This is another reason why I am glad it has been removed -- namely, because I believe that we are totally present in every cell of our body. You cannot have a "soul" -- or whatever you call it --without a body. The body is not something strange, but is the matter in which that which one could call soul is actual. Without this actuality it would not be real.

So, for all these reasons, I think, it is good that since Hume and Kant we have this immortal soul removed. Our relationship to the eternal is in no way dependent on this almost materialistic doctrine of a soul-substance besides our body-substance.

The Power of Being Over-coming Non-being

Question: Dr. Tillich, in your book, *The Courage To Be,* you analyzed the problem of maturity and self-discovery. My question is: what is the power which enables one constantly to overcome non-being in self-affirmation of being and in the process of *The Courage To Be*? How does one analyze the effects of the estrangement, alienation, and guilt, which bind one's own being? And this in relation to the New Being? And how does the Gestalt of Grace remove this alienation and estrangement?

Dr. Tillich: Now if I understood you, you had four questions. So I do not know whether I can get them all in my mind. Why don't you say the very first one.

Reply: The first one is: what is the "power" which enables being to overcome non-being in self-affirmation?

Dr. Tillich: Now there is first of all the vital power, which is a gift and which makes it possible for us to do the almost impossible things and to resist non-being in a really astonishing way. It exists in some situations of life, and these situations need this vitality.

But vitality is not everything. There is a courage which also comes from our ultimate concern. There is an interdependence between vitality and ultimate concern which you can observe. People who have a passionate eros towards something, passion for whatever it may be -- work to be done, for instance -- and love it (in Greek the word eros) develop more vitality. They have almost insuperable vitality in carrying through their work.

In situations where people do not hold or take anything so seriously -- perhaps one or two things but very few things -- and let life go on without being too much concerned about anything, they become devitalized. The vitality is vanishing. They often become either hysterical or neurotic. They are easily open to bodily attacks because the power of the ultimate concern in our centered self is not strong enough to carry them over many bodily attacks.

Now I have seen that in myself in periods in which the overwork was stupendous, but the eros towards what I had to do was great enough that nothing ever happened to me. I was healthy, and I remained healthy. In period when the eros disappears, which sometimes happens when the power of being is diminished, then one is open for passions and anxieties, which are not necessary, for bodily afflictions and even for accidents. The way in which our body immediately reacts against the danger of accidents is an expression of a love for something which is so great that unconsciously (of course) we want to preserve ourselves for it. If there is no such alert,then we are open to all these vicissitudes. That is a partial answer to your question. Now what was the second one?

The Effects of Estrangement and the New Being

Question: How do you analyze the effects of this estrangement, alienation, and guilt which bind one's being? This is in relation to the contrast with how do we free ourselves from the binding effects?

Dr. Tillich: I do not know whether I fully understand that. How do we do what?

Question: How do we analyze the effects of the estrangement and alienation which we find in ourselves? And when we see ourselves in this situation, in the New Being, how in the New Being do we overcome the alienation?

Dr. Tillich: Oh, I see. Now I think the first effect, which we already touched upon several times, and especially yesterday afternoon with the group of psychotherapists in Columbus, is the guilt experience. The main effect is the experience of guilt -- feeling of guilt -- because of estrangement. Estrangement means not acting according to what we essentially are, against our true nature. So we have guilt-feeling.

Allow me to say something here which again came out yesterday afternoon. The English word "guilt" has two meanings: namely, the objective "should," becoming guilty objectively by doing something which should not be done, culpi in that case; and also the feeling of guilt. This is very confusing. When the psychoanalysts, especially, or general psychotherapists speak of guilt -- "[one] has guilt" -- then they mean "[one] has guilt-feeling," but [one] might also have objective guilt. [One] might have done something terrible -- to [oneself] or to somebody else or to the order of life generally. Then [one] feels guilt, but [one] is also objectively guilty. So we should distinguish these two things and use different words for them.

Now the overcoming. If it is neurotic guilt-feeling, then, of course, we cay say then it is only guilt-feeling because the neurotic guilt-feeling refers to things which are not a real guilt. They produce guilt somewhere where it does not exist, in their imagination. I heard from a man who was analyzed that there was a feeling in him that he had killed his sister when both were around two years old. But this, of course, is a neurosis, which has other causes. There was no killing or anything like this, but it was a diversion from the real guilt-feeling -- where there is a real guilt, which I do not know, of course, but which can be found.

So the psychoanalyst can help us to overcome guilt-feelings which are unwanted. [One] cannot overcome the feeling of a bad conscience after real guilt. Here the religious comes in, namely, the message of forgiveness or of acceptance, if you want so, which does not necessarily come from God or from a higher being, but which does not come from the analyst and does not come from us, because the analyst needs it in every moment of [one's] life as equally as the patient needs it. It cannot come from analysis. The analysis can remove neurotic guilt-feelings, but the genuine ones can be overcome only by, let's say, mediation and prayer for forgiveness -- or so -- and by the acceptance that you are accepted. But this is a religious paradox.

THE CENTERED SELF

Question: This is a follow-up to the question asked about soul. It occurs to me that not only does soul go out the window with some psychological analyses but perhaps also the concept "self" and the "centered self" which you employ. I wonder if you could speak about the status of self as vis-as-vis the scientific psychology?

Dr. Tillich: Yes, I know that there is a tendency in some psychologies -- not in all -- to remove the "self." The immortal soul is removed by everybody but not the "self." In Jungian psychology the concept plays a very great role. It is also used in Freud, indirectly, when he speaks about the id, the ego, and the super ego; the ego, then, is the self.

You cannot escape the statement, which is merely a phenomenological statement without any theory involved in it, that "I am related to myself." This is a phenomenological description of a phenomenon as it appears to us, in us, in every moment in which we attack its existence. So it is simply self-deception, or it is a matter of language, if we exclude "self."

I had to give a lecture recently about the integration and the disintegration of the self. In this lecture I took your point of view into consideration and said that when I speak of the self, I do not want to replace the expelled soul by the self as a kind of thing -- a kind of additional reality. In reality we have the functions of our total personality in every moment. They include the bodily, the unconscious, the conscious, the spirit, our spirit, the mind, of course. All this is included in every moment. But all this is possible because we have that centeredness which makes it possible for us. These are events which happen in me.

As long as [people], even the analysts, say, "I am of the opinion that there is not an 'I,'" then they simply make self-deceptive and ultimately self-contradictory statements. But they can fully accept Kant's criticism -- Kant's paralogism, as he calls it -- made of the accompanying "I" consciousness. In every act of thinking we accompany it with the saying, "I am aware that I am thinking now." This accompanies every experience, but this cannot be put into an independent reality. It is the accompanying experience of the centered self.

I would criticize people who say there is no self simply in the question of terminology. I would say, "What do you mean with it? What do you mean the accompanying ego consciousness? If you really mean this, then you had better stop talking and go down, not into the animal status where that also exists, but into the vegetative status. If you were a flower, then you, of course, would not have a self-consciousness or ego-consciousness; but you are a [person], so you have it; and only because you have it, you can establish this absurd and self-destructive theory."

That would be my answer to this. But the self should not be dealt with as an independent reality beside the functions. It is present only in its function; in this I agree with the psychologists.

PERSONAL RELATIONSHIPS AND THE EXPERIENCE OF GOD

Question: Professor Tillich, Dr. Howe, in his book *Man's Need and God's Action*, says that a person experiences the love of God only in so far as [one] experiences other people loving [one]. Would you care to comment on that?

Dr. Tillich: Yes, I think it's wrong. But it is right in one thing. This brings us to a much larger problem.

Where does the personal self arise? How can it arise? It is a continuation of your question on the centered self and has bearing on your question on the power of being overcoming non-being. Interestingly enough, I discovered, lecturing day before yesterday about Fichte, the German philosopher,[6] how much he anticipated the famous Buber ego-thou relationship, which is the producer of our ego-consciousness -- of ourself as a person. In the same way Fichte says that only in the encounter of self-with-self is there self-growth. In the encounter, that which is potentially in every individual human being now becomes a personal self.

The reason for this is that we can use everything in nature as a tool; but if we use another person as a tool, then we overlook the fact that in [one's] being-a-person, [one] demands the same response that we demand; namely, to be acknowledged as a person, as a centered self. In doing so, we grow into a person. The other one is the only wall which no human being can pierce without ruining [oneself].

Hegel has expressed it beautifully in his section on master and slave, in *The Phenomenology of the Spirit,* where both are equally ruined. The master becomes dependent on the slave -- becomes the slave of the slave. The slave is deprived of [one's] centered personality -- or subjectivity, as Hegel says, but that is in another sense than we use the word.

This is the fundamental encounter in which the limit is put before every individual, which [one] can trespass. This absolute limit -- this unconditional demand -- is nothing else than the unconditional moral command.

So up to this point, I would say that our theoretical as well as our practical life is dependent on this experience. There is no possibility of having any experience in the realm of the spirit -- neither morality nor cultural creativity -- normally without this. This encounter causes a full encounter only if the other one is "taken in" and not only acknowledged in abstracto. And "taken in" means "taken in in love." Here I again follow you who has asked the question.

Now I would say, we have experiences with the ultimate which are, of course, to be expressed in analogy with our love experience between [people]. But this does not mean that they are dependent on this experience. The expression is dependent. We can say, "God is love," only because we have experienced love in relation to other human beings. By the way there is also a special form of love -- eros type of love -- towards nature. This is also independent of the person-to-person love. Through both nature and [humanity] something else can come to us, and then that something can appear independently of both of them.

Here is the problem which was discussed very much in the Ritschlian school of theology[7] during the latter half of the 19th century. In my student years the Ritschlian school was still the most influential. They said the same thing. They said it is mysticism to experience the love of God in the immediacy of our individual existence. Now this mysticophobia[8] of all Kantian schools and of the Ritschlian school has been overcome since the beginning of this century.

I do not know this book, but if it is as you describe it, it is a relapse to the moralism of the Kantian school in theology -- namely, the Ritschlian school. I would say, if you take away the mystical element -- namely, the presence of God -- out of religion, then it becomes a system of moral commands, as it has become in this country to a large extent. Now that is what I feel about this point.

But there is somebody who is so negative. I would like to hear your criticism of this.

Critic: Well, I . . .

Moderator: Excuse me, I think we are going to have to stop now for lunch. However, Dr. Tillich has graciously consented to linger for a little bit after the luncheon and perhaps you could raise your question with him at that time.

FOOTNOTES

1.   Originally published in *The Journal of Pastoral Care,* Vol. XXVI, No. 3, September 1972, pp. 176-189, with inclusive language added.

2.   Pythagoreans discovered that not only nature but mind could be expressed mathematically. They taught that the essence of all things was not water, nor fire, nor air, but Number, so that everything could be expressed numerically. They sought perfect harmony, equilibrium, and balance as the goal of life and the key to health. (H.E. Sigerist, *A History of Medicine,* vol. II. New York: Oxford University Press, 1961, pp. 94-99)

3. All the books of the Hippocratic collection of medical insight, which was based upon careful observation, wide personal experience, and reasoning, were written in Ionian Greek. "Why? Because Greek philosophy and Science were born in the Ionian colonies, not on the mainland, not in Athens, but on the coast of Asia Minor in the flourishing cities where Greek and Oriental civilizations came in close touch." While the Ionians sought to discover the substance that constituted everything. the Pythagoreans concentrated on eternal mathematical laws that ruled everything (H. E. Sigerist, op. cit., Pre-Socratic Philosophers and Early medical Schools, pp. 84-115)

4. Heraclitus, around 500 B.C., interpreted reality dynamically by teaching that the only permanence was change -- everything flows, nothing remains the same. Change was explained as the result of strife or tension. Harmony results from opposite tensions, and awareness of reality comes through opposites. Thus, everything carries with it its opposite -- disease and health, weariness and rest, being and non-being -- making the transitional state of becoming the only real one. For him, fire, not water, was the underlying substance of the universe. Life and reason were identified with fire. (H. E. Sigerist, op. cit., pp. 93-94)

5. Paralogism is defined as "a piece of false reasoning . . . a fallacy, esp . . . one of which the reasoner is [oneself] unconscious." (*The Oxford Universal Dictionary.* Oxford: Clarendon Press, 1955.) While Tillich refers quite correctly to Kant's paralogism of pure reason (I. Kant, *Critique of Pure Reason,* trans. by J. M. D. Meiklejohn. New York: Dutton and Co., 1950, pp. 233-249), his phraseology is taken more directly from Fichte: "Since all other consciousness is possible only under the condition of this immediate consciousness, it is obvious that this consciousness which is called I must accompany all my other conceptions, be necessarily contained in them, although not always clearly perceived by me, and that in each moment of consciousness I must refer everything to this I. . . ." (J. G. Fichte, *The Vocation of Man* [sic], edited by R. M. Chisholm. Indianapolis: The Liberal Arts Press, 1956, p. 79)

6.   Johann Gottlieb Fichte, 1762-1814. Fichte emphasized the active indivisible Ego as the source of the structure of knowledge. "What you assume to be a consciousness of an object is nothing but a consciousness of the fact that you have posited the object -- posited it necessarily, in accordance with an inward law of your thought, at the same time as the sensation" (p. 57). Consequently, the object that is supposed to exist is "a product of your own thought only." But, he reasons, we cannot experience ourselves any more directly than external objects. It follows, according to him, that the Ego must not only posit the existence of a non-Ego, but also the existence of itself as well, resulting in the thought of both an object and a subject accompanying sensations (pp. 60-62, 64).

The conception of beings like one's self produces from the voice of one's conscience the command, "'Here set a limit to your freedom; here recognize and honor purposes which are not your own.' . . . which is first translated . . . 'Here, certainly and truly, are beings like myself free and independent'" (p. 95). On the basis of further reasoning Fichte concludes that "free spirits" have "knowledge of free spirits," "only through" God. Respect for others' freedom comes from the command of conscience (pp. 136-137). (Fichte, *The Vocation of Man*[sic], op. cit.)

7.   Albrecht Ritschl, 1822-1889. Following Kant's breaking the stranglehold of a certain type of rationalism, the Ritschlian school of theology reacted against natural theology and rationalistic metaphysics. It stressed the centrality of ethics and the human community, while it also followed Kant in preserving considerable moral rationalism.

8.   Anti-mysticism, a pathological fear of any form of mysticism. Tillich's point is that the real weakness of Kantian and Ritschlian schools of thought was their elimination of the mystical participation element in religion.

ABOUT THE AUTHOR

Currently, Professor of Religion and Personality at Garrett-Evangelical Theological Seminary and an advisory member of the Graduate Faculty of Northwestern University in Evanston, Illinois. Previously, he spent ten years in parish ministry and served twenty-one years on the faculty of Colgate Rochester/Bexley Hall/Crozer Theological Schools in Rochester, New York.

In his efforts to understand the human psyche he has dissected brains and interpreted dreams. Further, he plants rock and woos dragons. Recently, he received a delivery of 3 1/2 tons of pebbles to be used in building a dry sea in his oriental garden.

As part of his consultation with church, educational, community, clinical, and governmental agencies, he served as a member of the Professional Task Force assembled by the Field Foundation in 1977 to engage in "The Ten Year Review of Hunger, Malnutrition, and Delivery of Health care in the United States.

He has written extensively for professional publications, such as, *Zygon, The Journal of Pastoral Care, Pastoral Psychology, The Christian Century, Foundations,* and *Religion in Life.* He serves on editorial boards of *The Journal of Pastoral Care, Review of Religious Research,* and *Journal of Pastoral Psychotherapy.* His latest book is *The Human Mind and the Mind of God;* theological promise in brain research. Among six previous books are *Christianity For Pious Skeptics* and *Responding to Human Pain.* He also has contribute chapters to five other books.

He received his B.A. from Denison University, which conferred upon him an Honorary Doctor of Laws degree in 1976. His theological education includes a B.D. from Colgate Rochester and graduate work at Union Theological Seminary in New York City. His psychological education includes an M.A. and Ph.D. from Ohio State University, plus clinical pastoral education in various settings. He is a Diplomate in the American Association of Pastoral Counselors and a Diplomate (sub-speciality clinical) in the American Board of Professional Psychology.

In 1987, the American Association of Pastoral Counselors and The Alumni/ae Association of the Institutes of Religion and Health each recognized him as "a pioneer in the field of pastoral psychotherapy."